In the Native State

IN THE
NATIVE STATE

Tom Stoppard

faber and faber
LONDON · BOSTON

First published in 1991
by Faber and Faber Limited
3 Queen Square London WCIN 3AU

Photoset by Wilmaset Birkenhead Wirral
Printed in Great Britain by
Clays Ltd, St Ives, plc

© Tom Stoppard, 1991

Tom Stoppard is hereby identified as author of this work in accordance with
Section 77 of the Copyright, Designs and Patents Act 1988.

All rights whatsoever in these plays are strictly reserved and professional
applications to perform them, etc., must be made in advance, before rehearsals
begin, to Fraser and Dunlop (Scripts) Limited, Fifth Floor, The Chambers,
Chelsea Harbour, London SW10 0XE, and amateur applications for permission to
perform them, etc., must be made in advance, before rehearsals begin, to
Samuel French Limited, 52 Fitzroy Street, London WIR 6JR

*This book is sold subject to the condition that it shall not, by way of trade
or otherwise, be lent, resold, hired out or otherwise circulated without the
publisher's prior consent in any form of binding or cover other than that
in which it is published and without a similar condition including
this condition being imposed on the subsequent purchaser.*

A CIP record for this book is available from the British Library

ISBN 0 571 16464 1

For Felicity Kendal

CHARACTERS

FLORA CREWE, aged thirty-five
NIRAD DAS, aged thirty-three
MRS SWAN, aged eighty-three
ANISH DAS, aged forty
DAVID DURANCE, about thirty, officer class
NAZRUL, young or middle-aged, a Muslim, speaks no
English
PIKE, age not crucial (thirty-five to fifty-five), educated
American, Southern accent
COOMARASWAMI, middle-aged, fat, cheerful; Indian accent
RESIDENT, aged forty-plus, Winchester and Cambridge
RAJAH, aged late fifties, educated at Harrow
NELL (Mrs Swan), aged twenty-three; middle-class
bluestocking
FRANCIS, say thirty-three, Indian Civil Service
EMILY EDEN (a real person), was forty-two in 1839

In addition
Indian QUESTIONER
Club SERVANT
English MAN and WOMAN at the Club

In the Native State was first transmitted on BBC Radio 3 on 21 April 1991. The cast was as follows:

FLORA CREWE	Felicity Kendal
NIRAD DAS	Sam Dastor
MRS SWAN	Peggy Ashcroft
ANISH DAS	Lyndam Gregory
NELL	Emma Gregory
DAVID DURANCE	Simon Treves
NAZRUL	Amerjit Deu
PIKE	William Hootkins
COOMARASWAMI	Renu Setnar
RESIDENT	Brett Usher
RAJAH	Saeed Jaffrey
FRANCIS/Englishman	Mark Straker
EMILY EDEN/Englishwoman	Auriol Smith
Directed by John Tydeman	

The play is set in two places and periods: India in 1930, and England in the present day.

We come to learn that Nirad Das was educated initially at a 'vernacular school', unlike Anish Das, who went to a 'convent school'. The significance of this is that Nirad speaks English with a stronger Indian accent than Anish.

*The verandah of a guesthouse. Jummapur would be a considerable
town, but the guesthouse is conceived as being set somewhat on its
own; the ambient sound would not be urban. There are references to
monkeys, parrots, dogs, chickens. The surround would be sandy, not
metalled.*

FLORA: (*Interior voice*)

> 'Yes, I am in heat like a bride in a bath,
> without secrets, soaked in heated air
> that liquifies to the touch and floods,
> shortening the breath, yes,
> I am discovered, heat has found me out,
> a stain that stops at nothing,
> not the squeezed gates or soft gutters,
> it brims as I shift,
> it webs my fingers round my pen,
> yes, think of a woman in a blue dress
> sat on a straight-backed chair at a plain table
> on the verandah of a guesthouse,
> writing about the weather.
> Or think, if you prefer, of bitches,
> cats, goats, monkeys at it like knives
> in the jacaranda – '

NIRAD DAS: Do you want me to stop, Miss Crewe?

FLORA: What?

DAS: Would you like to rest?

FLORA: No, I don't want to rest. Do you?

DAS: Not at all, but you crossed your legs, and I thought
perhaps –

FLORA: Oh! I'm so sorry! So I did. There. Is that how I was?

DAS: You are patient with me. I think your nature is very kind.

FLORA: Do you think so, Mr Das?

DAS: I am sure of it. May I ask you a personal question?

FLORA: That *is* a personal question.

DAS: Oh, my goodness, is it?

I

FLORA: I always think so. It always feels like one. *Carte blanche* is what you're asking, Mr Das. Am I to lay myself bare before you?

DAS: (*Panicking slightly*) My question was only about your poem!

FLORA: At least you knew it was personal.

DAS: I will not ask it now, of course.

FLORA: On that understanding I will answer it. My poem is about heat.

DAS: Oh. Thank you.

FLORA: I resume my pose. Pen to paper. Legs uncrossed. You know, you are the first man to paint my toenails.

DAS: Actually, I am occupied in the folds of your skirt.

FLORA: Ah. In that you are not the first.

DAS: You have been painted before? But of course you have! Many times, I expect!

FLORA: You know, Mr Das, your nature is much kinder than mine.

Interior. We come to learn that Mrs Swan is serving tea (on a brass table-top) in a bungalow in Shepperton, a garden's length from the (quiet) road.

MRS SWAN: Do you think you take after your father?

ANISH: I don't know. I would like to think so. But my father was a man who suffered for his beliefs, and I have never had to do that, so . . .

MRS SWAN: I meant being a painter. You are a painter like your father.

ANISH: Oh . . . yes. Yes, I am a painter like my father. Though not at all like my father, of course.

MRS SWAN: Your father was an Indian painter, you mean?

ANISH: An Indian painter? Well, I'm as Indian as he was. But yes. I suppose I am not a particularly *Indian* painter . . . not an Indian painter *particularly*, or rather . . .

MRS SWAN: Not particularly an Indian painter.

ANISH: Yes. But then, nor was he. Apart from being Indian.

MRS SWAN: As you are.

ANISH: Yes.

MRS SWAN: (*Pouring tea*) Though you are not at all like him.

ANISH: No. Yes. Perhaps if you had seen my work . . . (*Accepting the teacup.*) Oh, thank you.

MRS SWAN: Of course, *you* are a successful painter.

ANISH: I didn't mean that, Mrs Swan . . . only that my father was a quite different kind of artist, a portrait painter, as you know . . .

MRS SWAN: I can't say I do, Mr Das. Until I received your letter your father was unknown to me. In fact, the attribution 'unknown Indian artist' summed up the situation exactly, if indeed it was your father who made the portrait of my sister.

ANISH: Oh, the portrait is certainly my father's work, Mrs Swan! And I have brought the evidence to show you! I have been in such a state! I have done no work for a week!

3

You simply cannot imagine my feelings when I saw the book in the shop window – my excitement! You see, I carry my copy everywhere.

MRS SWAN: Well, I hope there'll be lots like *you*, Mr Das.

ANISH: There will be no one like me, Mrs Swan! It was not the book, of course, but the painting on the jacket and the same on the frontispiece inside! My father was not 'unknown' in Jummapur. Surely the publishers or somebody . . .

MRS SWAN: They made inquiries by letter, but it was all sixty years ago.

ANISH: Yes. If only my father could have known that one day his portrait of Flora Crewe would . . .

MRS SWAN: By the way, what *were* your father's beliefs?

ANISH: (*Surprised*) Why . . . we are Hindu . . .

MRS SWAN: You said he had suffered for his beliefs.

ANISH: Oh. I meant his opinions. For which he suffered imprisonment.

MRS SWAN: Who put him in prison?

ANISH: You did.

MRS SWAN: I did?

ANISH: I mean, the British.

MRS SWAN: Oh, I see. *We* did. But how did we know what his opinions were?

ANISH: Well . . . (*Uncertainly.*) I suppose he took part in various actions . . .

MRS SWAN: Then he was imprisoned for his actions not his opinions, Mr Das, and obviously deserved what he got. Will you have a slice of cake?

ANISH: Thank you.

MRS SWAN: Victoria sponge or Battenberg?

ANISH: Oh . . .

MRS SWAN: The sponge is my own, the raspberry jam too.

ANISH: I would love some.

(*A clock chimes in the room.*)

MRS SWAN: Ignore it. The clock has decided to be merely decorative. It chimes at random. There we are, then . . .

ANISH: Thank you.

4

MRS SWAN: But all that must have been before you were born
. . . Independence . . .

ANISH: Oh, yes, long before. I was the child of my father's
second marriage. I was born in '49, and these events took
place in Jummapur in 1930.

MRS SWAN: 1930! But that was when Flora was in Jummapur!

ANISH: Yes, I know. That is why I am here.

On the verandah.

FLORA: Mr Das, I am considering whether to ask you a delicate question, as between friends and artists.

DAS: Oh, Miss Crewe, I am transported beyond my most fantastical hopes of our fellowship! This is a red-letter day without dispute!

FLORA: If you are going to be so Indian I shan't ask it.

DAS: But I cannot be less Indian than I am.

FLORA: You could if you tried. I'm not sure I'm going to ask you now.

DAS: Then you need not, dear Miss Crewe! You considered. The unasked, the almost asked question, united us for a moment in its intimacy, we came together in your mind like a spark in a vacuum glass, and the redness of the day's letter will not be denied.

FLORA: You are still doing it, Mr Das.

DAS: You wish me to be less Indian?

FLORA: I did say that but I think what I meant was for you to be *more* Indian, or at any rate *Indian*, not Englished-up and all over me like a labrador and knocking things off tables with your tail – so *waggish* of you, Mr Das, to compare my mind to a vacuum. You only do it with us. I don't believe that left to yourself you can't have an ordinary conversation without jumping backwards through hoops of delight, *with* whoops of delight, I think I mean; actually, I do know what I mean, I want you to be with me as you would be if *I* were Indian.

DAS: An Indian Miss Crewe! Oh dear, that is a mental construction which has no counterpart in the material world.

FLORA: A *unicorn* is a mental construction which has no counterpart in the material world but you can imagine it.

DAS: You can imagine it but you cannot mount it.

FLORA: Imagining it was all I was asking in my case.

6

DAS: (*Terribly discomfited*) Oh! Oh, my gracious! I had no intention – I assure you –

FLORA: (*Amused*) No, no, you cannot unwag your very best wag. You cleared the table, the bric-à-brac is on the parquet – the specimen vase, the snuff box, the souvenir of Broadstairs – (*But she has misjudged.*)

DAS: (*Anguished*) You are cruel to me, Miss Crewe!

FLORA: (*Instantly repentant*) Oh! I'm so sorry. I didn't want to be. It's my nature. Please come out from behind your easel – look at me.

DAS: May we fall silent, please. I prefer to work in silence.

FLORA: I've spoiled everything. I'm very sorry.

DAS: The shadow has moved. I must correct it.

FLORA: Yes, it has moved. It cannot be corrected. We must wait for tomorrow. I'm so sorry.

ANISH: When my father met Flora Crewe he had been a widower for several years, although he was still quite a young man, a year or two younger than her, yes . . . the beginning of the Hot Weather in 1930: he would have been not yet thirty-four. He had lost his wife to cholera and he was childless. I knew nothing of my father's life before Swaraj. The British Empire was prehistory to me. By the time I was old enough to be curious, my father was over sixty, an old gentleman who spoke very little except when he sometimes read aloud to me. I say read to me but really he read to himself, with me in attendance. He liked to read in English. Robert Browning, Tennyson, Macaulay's *Lays of Ancient Rome*, and Dickens, of course . . .

MRS SWAN: How surprising.

ANISH: Oh, yes. (*Meaning 'no'.*) He went from a vernacular school to Elphinstone College in Bombay, and you only have to look at Elphinstone College to know it was built to give us a proper British education.

MRS SWAN: I really meant, how surprising in view of his 'opinions'. But I spoke without thinking. Your father resented the British and loved English literature, which was prefectly consistent of him, and I have interrupted you. You haven't mentioned your mother.

ANISH: My mother speaks no English. She is from a village, peasant farmers, no, plot-holders. She was born in the year Flora Crewe came to Jummapur, and she married when she was sixteen. It was not from her that I learned . . . that . . .

MRS SWAN: That . . . ?

ANISH: That my father was a thorn in the flesh of the British; and was still remembered for it – I might say, is honoured for it.

MRS SWAN: By whom?

ANISH: By his son.

MRS SWAN: It does you credit.

ANISH: In Bengal and the United Provinces, all over British India, of course, there were thousands of people who did as much and more, and went to gaol, but in Jummapur we were 'loyal', as you would say, we had been loyal to the British right through the First War of Independence.

MRS SWAN: The . . . ? What war was that?

ANISH: The Rising of 1857.

MRS SWAN: Oh, you mean the Mutiny. *What* did you call it?

ANISH: Dear Mrs Swan, imperial history is only the view from . . . no, no – please let us not argue. I promise you I didn't come to give you a history lesson.

MRS SWAN: You seem ill-equipped to do so. We were your Romans, you know. We might have been your Normans.

ANISH: And did you expect us to be grateful?

MRS SWAN: That's neither here nor there. I don't suppose I'd have been grateful if a lot of Romans turned up and started laying down the law and the language and telling us we were all one country now, so Wessex had to stop fighting Mercia, and so forth. 'What a cheek,' is probably what I would have thought. 'Go away, and take your roads and your baths with you.' It doesn't matter what I would have thought. It's what I think now that matters. You speak English better than most young people I meet. Did you go to school here?

ANISH: No, I went to a convent school in . . . You are spreading a net for me, Mrs Swan.

MRS SWAN: What net would that be? Have some more cake.

ANISH: Mrs Swan, you are a very wicked woman. You advance a preposterous argument and try to fill my mouth with cake so I cannot answer you. I will resist you and your cake. *We* were the Romans! We were up to date when you were a backward nation. The foreigners who invaded *you* found a third-world country! Even when you discovered India in the age of Shakespeare, we already had our Shakespeares. And our science, architecture, our literature and art, we had a culture older and more splendid, we were rich! After all, that's why you came. (*But he has misjudged.*)

9

MRS SWAN: (*Angrily*) We made you a proper country! And when we left you fell straight to pieces like Humpty Dumpty! Look at the map! You should feel nothing but shame!

ANISH: Oh, yes . . . I am ashamed. I am a guest in your house and I have been . . .

MRS SWAN: . . . no, only provocative. We will change the subject.

ANISH: I'm sorry.

(*The clock chimes.*)

MRS SWAN: That clock has gone quite mad. It has gained twenty minutes since this morning . . . There seems no point in putting it back.

ANISH: No, we cannot put it back. I'm so sorry.

FLORA: While having tiffin on the verandah of my bungalow I spilled kedgeree on my dungarees and had to go to the gymkhana in my pyjamas looking like a coolie.

DAS: I was buying chutney in the bazaar when a thug who had escaped from the choky ran amuck and killed a box-wallah for his loot, creating a hullabaloo and landing himself in the mulligatawny.

FLORA: I went doolally at the durbar and was sent back to Blighty in a dooley feeling rather dikki with a cup of char and a chit for a chotapeg.

DAS: Yes, and the burra sahib who looked so pukka in his topi sent a coolie to the memsahib —

FLORA: No, no. You can't have memsahib *and* sahib, that's cheating – and anyway, I've already said coolie.

DAS: I concede, Miss Crewe. You are the Hobson-Jobson champion!

FLORA: You are chivalrous, Mr Das. So I'll confess I had help. I found a whole list of Anglo-Indian words in my bedside drawer, for the benefit of travellers.

DAS: But I know both languages, so you still win on handicap.

FLORA: Where did you learn everything, Mr Das?

DAS: From books. I like Dickens and Browning and Shakespeare of course – but my favourite is Agatha Christie! *The Mysterious Affair at Styles*! Oh, the woman is a genius! But I would like to write like Macaulay.

FLORA: Oh dear.

DAS: I have to thank Lord Macaulay for English, you know. It was his idea when he was in the government of India that English should be taught to us all. He wanted to supply the East India Company with clerks, but he was sowing dragon's teeth. Instead of babus he produced lawyers, journalists, civil servants – he produced Gandhi! We have so many, many languages, you know, that English is the only language the nationalists can communicate in! That is a very good joke on Macaulay, don't you think?

FLORA: Are *you* a nationalist, Mr Das?

DAS: Ah, that is a very interesting question! But we shouldn't have stopped. It's getting late for you. I must work more quickly.

FLORA: It's only half-past ten.

DAS: No, it's nearly April, and that is becoming late.

FLORA: Yes, it seems hotter than ever. Would you like some more lemonade?

DAS: No, thank you, no lemonade. Miss Crewe, you haven't looked at my painting yet.

FLORA: No. Not yet. I never look. Do you mind?

DAS: No.

FLORA: You do really. But I once asked a painter, 'Can I look?' and he said, 'Why? When I paint a table I don't have to show it to the table.'

DAS: I said you had been painted before.

FLORA: Only once.

DAS: A portrait?

FLORA: Not in the way you mean. It was a nude.

DAS: Oh.

FLORA: Unusually. He painted his friends clothed. For nudes he used models. I believe I was his friend. But perhaps not. Perhaps a used model only. It hardly matters. He was dead so soon afterwards. He was not so kind to me as you are. I had to lie with my shoulders flat but my hips twisted towards the canvas; I could hardly move afterwards.

DAS: Do you have the painting?

FLORA: No.

DAS: Where is it?

FLORA: Nowhere. A man I thought I might marry destroyed it. So after that, I didn't want to be painted again.

DAS: Oh . . .

FLORA: But luckily I forgot that, when you asked me. I must have got over it without realizing. My goodness, what a red-letter day you are having. There's a man on a horse.

DURANCE: (*Off*) Good morning! Miss Crewe, I think!

FLORA: Yes, good morning! (*Aside to* DAS.) Do you know him?
    (*To* DURANCE.) How do you do!
DAS: He is the Assistant.
DURANCE: (*Off*) May I get down a moment?
FLORA: Of course. What a beautiful animal! (*Aside to* DAS.)
    Assistant what?
DAS: Captain Durance!
DURANCE: Thank you!
FLORA: Come on up, do join us.
    (*We have heard the horse walking forward, perhaps snorting,
    and* DURANCE *dismounting, and now coming up the three or
    four wooden steps on to the verandah.*)
DURANCE: (*Arriving*) Oh, it's Mr Das, isn't it?
DAS: Good morning, sir. But we have never met.
DURANCE: Oh, but I know you. And Miss Crewe, your fame
    precedes you.
FLORA: Thank you . . . but . . .
DURANCE: I'm from the Residency. David Durance.
FLORA: How do you do?
DURANCE: Oh, but look here – I'm interrupting the artist.
FLORA: We had stopped.
DURANCE: May one look? Oh, I say! Coming along jolly well!
    Don't you think so, Miss Crewe?
DAS: I must be going. I have overstayed my time today.
FLORA: But we'll continue tomorrow?
DAS: Yes. Perhaps a little earlier if it suits you. I will leave
    everything just inside the door, if that is all right . . . and
    the easel . . . (DAS *is moving the objects, bumping them down
    in the interior.*)
FLORA: Yes, of course. Why don't you leave the canvas too? It
    will be quite safe.
DAS: I . . . yes . . . I have a drape for it. Thank you. There.
FLORA: Like shutting up the parrot for the night.
DAS: There we are. Thank you for the lemonade, Miss Crewe.
    An absolute treat. I promise you! Goodbye, sir – and –
    yes – and until tomorrow . . . (*He goes down the steps to the
    outside and mounts a bicycle and pedals away.*)
FLORA: Yes . . . goodbye! (*To* DURANCE.) I'll put my shoes on.

13

Sorry about my toes, but I like to wriggle them when I'm working.

DURANCE: I'll only stay a moment. My chief asked me to look in. Just to make sure there's nothing we can do for you.

FLORA: There's a servant who seems to come with the guesthouse, though he has a way of disappearing, but would you like some tea?

DURANCE: No, nothing for me. Really. We might have found you more comfortable quarters, you know, not quite so in-the-town.

FLORA: How did you know I was here?

DURANCE: Now there's a point. Usually we know of arrivals because the first thing they do is drop in a card, but in your case . . . rumours in the bazaar, so to speak. Are you an old hand here, Miss Crewe?

FLORA: No, I've never been to India before. I came up from Bombay just a few days ago.

DURANCE: But you have friends here, perhaps?

FLORA: No. I got on a boat and I came, knowing no one. I have friends in England who have friends here. Actually, one friend.

DURANCE: In Jummapur, this friend?

FLORA: No – the *friend* – my friend – is in London, of course; *his* friends are in different places in Rajputana, and I will also be going to Delhi and then up to the Punjab, I hope.

DURANCE: Now I see. And your friend in London has friends in Jummapur?

FLORA: Yes.

DURANCE: Like Mr Das?

FLORA: No. Are you a policeman of some kind, Mr Durance?

DURANCE: Me? No. I'm sorry if I sound like one.

FLORA: Well, you do a bit. I'm travelling with letters of introduction from Mr Joshua Chamberlain to a number of social clubs and literary societies. I speak on the subject of 'Literary Life in London', in return for board and lodging . . . So you see I couldn't have taken advantage of your kindness without giving offence to my hosts.

DURANCE: The game is different here. By putting up at the Residency you would have gained respect, not lost it.

FLORA: Thank you, but what about *self* respect?

DURANCE: Well . . . as long as all is well. So you are following in Chamberlain's footsteps. All is explained.

FLORA: I don't think *I* explained it. But yes, I am. He spoke in Jummapur three years ago, on the subject of Empire.

DURANCE: Yes. Is he a good friend?

FLORA: Yes.

DURANCE: Did you know he was some sort of Communist?

FLORA: I thought he might be. He stood twice for Parliament as the Communist candidate.

DURANCE: (*Unoffended, pleasant as before*) I amuse you. That's all right, amusing our distinguished visitors is among my duties.

FLORA: Well, don't be so stuffy. And call again if you like.

DURANCE: Thank you. How long will you be with us?

FLORA: I'm expected in Jaipur but they don't mind when I come.

DURANCE: I'm sure you'll have a marvellous time. There are wonderful things to see. Meanwhile, please consider yourself an honorary member of the Club – mention my name, but I'll put you in the book.

FLORA: Thank you.

DURANCE: Well . . .

FLORA: I wish I had a lump of sugar for your horse. Next time.

DURANCE: He's my main indulgence. I wish I'd been here when a good horse went with the job.

FLORA: Yes . . . what *is* your job? You mentioned your chief.

DURANCE: The Resident. He represents the government here.

FLORA: The British government?

DURANCE: Delhi. The Viceroy, in fact. Jummapur is not British India . . . you understand that?

FLORA: Yes . . . but it's all the Empire, isn't it?

DURANCE: Oh, yes. Absolutely. But there's about five hundred rajahs and maharajahs and nabobs and so on who run bits of it, well, nearly half of it actually, by treaty. And we're here to make sure they don't get up to mischief.

FLORA: I knew you were a kind of policeman.

DURANCE: (*Laughs*) Miss Crewe, would you have dinner with us while you are here?

FLORA: With you and your wife, do you mean?

DURANCE: No . . . at the Club. Us. With me. I don't run to a wife, I'm afraid. But do come. We're a reasonably civilized lot, and there's usually dancing on Saturdays; only a gramophone but lots of fun.

FLORA: I'd love to. On Saturday, then.

DURANCE: Oh . . . splendid! I'll come by. (*He mounts his horse.*)

FLORA: I haven't got a horse, you know.

DURANCE: We have a Daimler at the Residency. I'll see if I can wangle it. Pick you up about eight?

FLORA: Yes.

DURANCE: We don't dress, normally, except on dress nights. (*Laughs at himself.*) Obviously.

FLORA: I'll be ready.

DURANCE: Jolly good.

FLORA: Goodbye.

DURANCE: Goodbye.

FLORA: (*Calling out*) Wangle the Daimler!

ANISH: I apologize if I was rude. *You* didn't put my father in
   gaol, after all.

MRS SWAN: Not in any sense. Jummapur was a native state, so
   your father was put in gaol by his own people.

ANISH: (*Cautiously*) Well . . .

MRS SWAN: (*Firmly*) Whatever your father may have done, the
   Resident would have had no authority to imprison an
   Indian. The Rajah of Jummapur had his own justice.

ANISH: Even so, you – (*corrects himself*) the British . . .

MRS SWAN: Oh, I'm not saying we wouldn't have boxed his ears
   and sent him packing if he forgot which side his bread was
   buttered, but facts are facts. The Rajah put your father in
   the choky. How long for, by the way?

ANISH: Six months, actually.

MRS SWAN: There you are. In Bengal or the UP he would have
   got a year at least. After the war it may have been different.
   With Independence round the corner, people were queuing
   up to go to prison; it was their ticket to the show. They'd
   do their bit of civil disobedience and hop into the paddy-
   wagon thoroughly pleased with themselves. Francis – that's
   my husband – would let them off with a small fine if he
   thought they were Johnny-come-latelies, and they'd be
   furious. That was when Francis had his District. We were
   right up near Nepal . . .

ANISH: Yes, I noticed your . . .

MRS SWAN: Of course you did. In India we had pictures of
   coaching inns and fox hunting, and chintz covers from
   Liberty's and all sorts of knick-knackery from home . . .
   and now I've landed up in Shepperton I've got elephants
   and prayer-wheels cluttering up the window ledges, and the
   tea table is Nepalese brass. One could make a comment
   about human nature, but have a slice of Battenberg instead.

ANISH: Thank you.

MRS SWAN: I got it specially, an artistic sort of cake, I always think. What kind of paintings are they, these paintings that are not like your father's? Describe your latest. Like the cake?

ANISH: (*Eating*) Delicious. Thank you.

MRS SWAN: No, are they like the cake?

ANISH: Oh. No. They are all . . . like each other really. I can't *describe* them.

MRS SWAN: Indescribable, then. But modern, I suppose?

ANISH: (*Becoming slightly impatient*) It's not *my* paintings I have come about.

MRS SWAN: No, of course. You recognized your father's work in the window of a bookshop. Still, he might have been more pleased to be in one art gallery than in a hundred bookshops.

ANISH: Perhaps not. I'm sure my father never had a single one of his paintings reproduced, and that is an extraordinary pleasure for an artist. I know! The painting under one's hand is everything, of course . . . unique. But replication! *That* is popularity! If we are allowed a little worldly pride, put us on thousands and thousands of book jackets – on calendars – biscuit tins!

MRS SWAN: Well, it's only *three* thousand of the *Selected Letters*, but America is still to come. Mr Pike thinks Flora's letters will do very well in America, and he should know, being an American himself.

ANISH: Mr Pike?

MRS SWAN: The editor. He put the book together. A serious man, Mr Pike, with a surprising *Gone with the Wind* sort of accent.

ANISH: Editor? Oh, yes. So he is. 'Edited with an introduction by Eldon Cooper Pike.' What does it mean – edited – exactly? Are there more letters that are not in the book?

MRS SWAN: Naturally. *Selected Letters of Flora Crewe*, that is what it means. And then there's the footnotes. Mr Pike did those too.

ANISH: Oh yes . . . the footnotes.

MRS SWAN: Far too much of a good thing, the footnotes, in my opinion; to be constantly interrupted in a Southern drawl by someone telling you things you already know or don't need to know at that moment. I hear Mr Pike's voice every time I go to the bits at the bottom of the page. He teaches Flora Crewe at a university in Maryland. It makes her sound like a subject, doesn't it? Like biology, or in her case, botany. Flora is widely taught in America. I have been written to, even visited, and on one occasion telephoned, by young women doing Flora Crewe.

ANISH: Always young women?

MRS SWAN: Almost always, yes. She has become quite a heroine. Which she always was to me. I was only five when Mother died, so it was Flora who . . . oh dear, I'm going to need a hanky.

ANISH: Oh, I say! I'm sorry if I –

MRS SWAN: (*Snuffling*) Found it. (*She blows her nose.*) It makes me so cross that she missed it all, the *Collected Poems*, and now the *Letters*, with her name all over the place and students and professors so *interested* and so sweet about her poetry. Nobody gave tuppence about her while she was alive except to get her knickers off. Never mind, how is your tea?

ANISH: Erm . . . sorry. Very nice, very nice tea.

MRS SWAN: I'll have to go and repair myself. Yes, I like it well enough but I can't get the tea here to taste as it should. I expect it's the water. A reservoir near Staines won't have the makings of a good cup of tea compared to the water we got in the Hills. It came straight off the Himalayas. (*With the help of a stick she has walked to the door and closed it behind her.*)

FLORA: (*Interior voice*)

> 'Yes, I am in heat like a corpse in a ditch,
> my skin stained and porous as a photograph
> under a magnifying lens that shows each hair
> a lily stem straggling out of a poisoned swamp.
> Heat has had its way with me,
> yes, I know this ditch, I have been left for dead before,
> my lips gone slack and the wild iris
> flickers in the drooling cavity, insects
> crawl like tears from behind my eyes – '

Oh, fiddlesticks! May we stop for a moment. (*She gets up.*) I'm sticking to myself.

DAS: Of course! Forgive me!

FLORA: You musn't take responsibility for the climate too, Mr Das.

DAS: No, I . . .

FLORA: No, I'm sorry. I'm bad-tempered. Should we have some tea? I wouldn't mind something to eat too. (*Calls out.*) Nazrul! Am I saying his name right? There's a jar of duck pâté in the refrigerator . . .

(NAZRUL *is a male servant. He speaks Urdu.*)

Oh, Nazrul . . . char and . . .

NAZRUL: (*In Urdu*) Yes, madam, I will bring tea immediately . . .

FLORA: . . . bread . . . and in the fridge, no, don't go, listen to me –

DAS: Would you allow me, please?

(DAS *and* NAZRUL *speak in Urdu.* DAS *orders bread and butter and the duck pâté from the fridge. But* NAZRUL *has dramatic and tragic disclosures to make. Thieves have stolen the pâté.* DAS *berates him.*)

FLORA: (*Over the conversation*) . . . a jar with a picture of a duck . . .

(NAZRUL *is promising to fetch bread and butter and cake, and he leaves.*)
What was all that?

DAS: He will bring tea, and bread and butter and cake. The pâté has been taken by robbers.

FLORA: What?

DAS: (*Gravely*) Just so, I'm afraid.

FLORA: But the fridge is padlocked. Mr Coomaraswami pointed it out to me particularly.

DAS: Where do you keep the key?

FLORA: Nazrul keeps it, of course.

DAS: Ah well . . . the whole thing is a great mystery.
(FLORA *splutters into laughter and* DAS *joins in.*)

FLORA: But surely, isn't it against his religion?

DAS: Oh, certainly. I should say so. Not that I'm saying Nazrul stole the pâté, but stealing would be against his religion, undoubtedly.

FLORA: I don't mean stealing, I mean the pork.

DAS: But I thought you said it was duck.

FLORA: One must read the small print, Mr Das. 'Duck pâté' in large letters, 'with pork' in small letters. It's normal commercial practice.

DAS: Yes, I see.

FLORA: We must hope he only got the duck part . . .

DAS: That is your true nature speaking, Miss Crewe!

FLORA: . . . though of course, if they use one pig for every duck, Nazrul will have been lucky to get any duck at all.

DAS: The truth will never be known, only to God, who is merciful.

FLORA: Yes. Which God do you mean?

DAS: Yours if you wish, by all means.

FLORA: Now, Mr Das, there is such a thing as being too polite. Yours was here first.

DAS: Oh, but we Hindus can afford to be generous; we have gods to spare, one for every occasion. And Krishna said, 'Whichever god a man worships, it is I who answer the prayer.'

FLORA: I wasn't sure whether Krishna was a god or a person.

21

DAS: Oh, he was most certainly a god, one of the ten incarnations of Vishnu, and a favourite subject of the old Rajasthani painters. He had a great love affair, you see, with a married lady, Radha, who was the most beautiful of the herdswomen. Radha fell passionately in love with Krishna and she would often escape from her husband to meet him in secret.

FLORA: I think that's what confused me. Come and sit down, Mr Das. Take the cane chair. I'll keep mine for posture.

DAS: (*Sitting*) Thank you.

FLORA: I've been looking at temples with Mr Coomaraswami.

DAS: Yes. Do you find them interesting?

FLORA: I like some of the sculptures. The women have such serene faces. I mean, the goddesses.

DAS: Yes, they are beautiful.

FLORA: Breasts like melons, and baby-bearing hips. You must think me ill-favoured.

DAS: No. My wife was slightly built.

FLORA: Oh . . .

(NAZRUL *arrives with a noisy tray.*)

Thank you, Nazrul. Two kinds of cake!

(NAZRUL *leaves, saying in Urdu that he will return with bread and butter.*)

DAS: He will return with bread and butter.

FLORA: (*Arranging teacups*) How is your painting today?

DAS: Altered. Your face . . . I think your work was troublesome.

FLORA: Yes.

DAS: Is it the rhyming that is difficult?

FLORA: No.

DAS: The metre?

FLORA: No. The . . . emotion won't harmonize. I'm afraid I'm not much good at talking about it.

DAS: I'm sorry.

FLORA: That's why I don't keep nipping round to your side of the easel. If I don't look there's nothing to say. I think that that's better.

DAS: Yes. It is better to wait. My painting has no *rasa* today.

22

FLORA: What is *rasa*?

DAS: *Rasa* is juice. Its taste. Its essence. A painting must have its *rasa* . . . which is not *in* the painting exactly. *Rasa* is what you must feel when you see a painting, or hear music; it is the emotion which the artist must arouse in you.

FLORA: And poetry? Does a poem have *rasa*?

DAS: Oh yes! Without *rasa* it is not a poem, only words. That is a famous dictum of Vishvanata, a great teacher of poetry, six hundred years ago.

FLORA: *Rasa* . . . yes. My poem has no *rasa*.

DAS: Or perhaps it has two *rasas* which are in conflict.

FLORA: Oh . . .

DAS: There are nine *rasas*, each one a different colour. I should say mood. But each mood has its colour – white for laughter and fun, red for anger, grey for sorrow . . . each one has its own name, and its own god, too.

FLORA: And some don't get on. Is that it?

DAS: Yes. That is it. Some do and some don't. If you arouse emotions which are in opposition to each other the *rasas* will not . . . harmonize, you said.

FLORA: Yes.

DAS: Your poem is about heat.

FLORA: Yes.

DAS: But its *rasa* is perhaps . . . anger?

FLORA: Sex.

DAS: (*Unhesitatingly*) The *rasa* of erotic love is called Shringara. Its god is Vishnu, and its colour is *shyama*, which is blue-black. Vishvanata in his book on poetics tells us: Shringara requires, naturally, a lover and his loved one, who may be a courtesan if she is sincerely enamoured, and it is aroused by, for example, the moon, the scent of sandalwood, or being in an empty house. Shringara goes harmoniously with all other *rasas* and their complementary emotions, with the exception of cruelty, disgust and sloth.

FLORA: I see. Thank you. Empty house is very good. Mr Das, you sounded just like somebody else. Yourself, I expect. I knew you could. The other one reminded me of Dr Aziz in

Forster's novel. Have you read it yet? I kept wanting to kick him.

DAS: (*Offended*) Oh . . .

FLORA: For not knowing his worth.

DAS: Then perhaps you didn't finish it.

FLORA: Yes, perhaps. Does he improve?

DAS: He alters.

FLORA: What is your opinion of *A Passage to India*?

DAS: Was that the delicate question you considered to ask me?

FLORA: (*Laughs happily*) Oh, Mr Das!

MRS SWAN *re-enters the room.*

MRS SWAN: There . . . that's better . . .

ANISH: I was looking at your photographs. I hope you don't mind.

MRS SWAN: I took that one myself, in Venice, the summer before Flora went to India. I had a Kodak which let down in front in pleats. It took very good snaps; I wonder what happened to it? That was the day Diaghilev died. But we didn't know that till afterwards. We crossed to the Lido to have dinner with him at the hotel and he was dead.

ANISH: Is this one your husband?

MRS SWAN: Yes. That's Francis in Rawalpindi before we were married. Have you been up there?

ANISH: No. We have always lived in Rajasthan.

MRS SWAN: But you do not live there now?

ANISH: No. I live here now.

MRS SWAN: You wrote from St John's Wood.

ANISH: Yes. London is my home now. I have spent half my life here. I married here.

MRS SWAN: An English girl?

ANISH: Yes. Australian.

MRS SWAN: What an odd reply.

ANISH: Yes. I suppose so. Mrs Swan, it says in the book that your sister's portrait is reproduced by your permission. Does that mean you have it?

MRS SWAN: Yes.

ANISH: Here? In the house?

MRS SWAN: Oh, yes. Would you like to see it?

ANISH: Very much! I half expected to see it the moment I entered.

MRS SWAN: Pride of place, you thought. That's because you're a painter. Flora would not have cared to be on show. The portrait has always fended for itself rather . . .

ANISH: I understand. Where do you keep it?

MRS SWAN: Nowhere particularly. We always took it around with us from house to house and sometimes it ended up on top of a wardrobe. Oh dear, that must seem rather rude.

ANISH: It's all right.

MRS SWAN: Come along. It's in the bedroom, wrapped up. You're lucky. It only just came back from being photographed for the book. You can unwrap it for me. Where's my stick? Has it fallen down?

ANISH: Here . . . let me . . .

MRS SWAN: Thank you.

ANISH: Do you need me to help you?

MRS SWAN: I hope not. Otherwise what would I do when you'd gone? But you may open the door. You can see why I got a bungalow.

(*They are moving now, she with her stick. They enter another room.*)

I wonder what we called bungalows before India, and verandahs and so on. It must have made certain conversations quite awkward. 'I'm looking for a house with no upstairs and an outside-inside bit stuck on the front . . .'

Well, there you are! Rather well wrapped up. Will you need the kitchen scissors, do you think?

ANISH: We'll see. What is in the boxes?

MRS SWAN: Flora's letters. Mr Pike had them photographed too. Try to save the brown paper – it looks a good size to be useful.

ANISH: Yes, I will . . .

MRS SWAN: Oh, it's quite easy . . . that's it . . .

(*The painting is unwrapped.*)

Well, there she is.

ANISH: Oh . . .

MRS SWAN: Yes, a bit much, isn't it?

ANISH: Oh . . . it's . . . so vibrant . . .

MRS SWAN: Vibrant. Yes . . . Oh . . . I say, *you're* not going to blub too, are you?

ANISH: (*Weeping*) I'm sorry.

MRS SWAN: Don't worry. Borrow my hanky . . . It just goes to show, you need an eye. And your father, after all, was, like you, an Indian painter.

FLORA: 'Jummapur. April 5th. Darling Nell, I'm having my portrait painted by an artist I met here, and I'm not using the historical present, I mean he's at it as I write, so if you see a painting of me in my cornflower dress sitting writing on a verandah you'll know I was writing *this* – some of the time anyway. He thinks I'm writing a poem. Posing as a poet, you see, just as the Enemy once said of me in his rotten rag.'

(PIKE's *voice, which does sound rather like Clark Gable in* Gone with the Wind, *comes in immediately, intimate and slightly hushed, rather in the manner of the continuity voice which introduces live concerts on the radio.*)

PIKE: 'The Enemy' was J.C. Squire (1884–1958), poet, critic, literary editor of the *New Statesman*, and editor of the London *Mercury*. FC is evidently referring to an anonymous editorial in the London *Mercury* (April 1920) complaining about, 'an outbreak of versifying flappers who should stop posing as poets and confine themselves to posing as railway stations'. The magazine was sued by the poets Elizabeth Paddington (1901–88) and Lavinia Clapham (1899–1929), both cases being settled out of court. FC poured a pint of beer over Squire's head in the Fitzroy Tavern in January 1921.

FLORA: 'I am installed in a little house with a verandah and three good-sized rooms under a tin roof. The verandah is at the front and you go into the main room which has an electric ceiling-fan and electric light, and an oil lamp which I prefer even when the electricity hasn't failed. There's a nice big window at the back, looking out at a rather hopeless garden, and then there is a nice plain bedroom with a big bed and a desk and one wooden chair and a wash-stand, and through another door a little bathroom with a Victorian bath and also a shower which is, alas, contemporary makeshift. Over on the other side is a kitchen bit with a fridge, but my cook and bottle-washer disregards the electric stove and makes his own arrangements on a little verandah of his own. And all this is under a big green tree with monkeys and parrots in the branches and it's called a duck bungalow – '

PIKE: Dak bungalow, literally post-house.

FLORA: ' – although there is not a duck to be seen, only some scrawny chickens and a peahen. This is my first proper stop since I got off the boat and posted my Bombay letter. Yours overtook me and was waiting for me – why didn't I think of posting myself overland? – and thank you for it, but, darling, you musn't expect me to be Intelligence from Abroad, as the *Times* used to say – you obviously know much more than I do about the Salt March – '

PIKE: Gandhi's 'March to the Sea' to protest the salt tax began at Ahmedabad on March 12th. He reached the sea on the day this letter was written.

FLORA: ' – nobody has mentioned it to me – and you'd better explain to Josh that the earthshaking sensations of Lord Beaverbrook's new Empire Party, etc. – '

PIKE: See Appendix G.

FLORA: ' – cause little stir in Jummapur. Sorry to disappoint.' (*The appropriate sound effects creep in to illustrate Flora's letter, so here we begin to hear a slow steam train, followed in due course by the hubbub of the station, the clip-clop of the horse pulling the buggy as mentioned and the bicycle bells etc. which accompany the ride into town. Further down the letter, it is intended that Flora's questioner at her lecture will be heard in the appropriate physical ambience. In general, Flora's letter becomes an immediate presence – we can hear her pen scratching now and then, and insects, distant life, etc. – but when her letter takes us into an event, the sound-plot turns into the appropriate accompaniment.*)

'I arrived here on a huffing and puffing local with as many people riding on the roof as inside, and the entire committee of the Jummapur Theosophical Society was on the platform, bunch of flowers at the ready, not quite a red carpet and brass band but almost, and I thought there must

be someone important on the train and it turned out to be
me – '

COOMARASWAMI: Miss Crewe! Welcome to Jummapur!

FLORA: Thank you! Now nice!

'– which was very agreeable.'

Are you Mr Coomaraswami?

COOMARASWAMI: That is me! Is this suitcase your only
luggage?

FLORA: 'And in no time at all they put me in a buggy and the
President of the Theosophical sat beside me holding a
yellow parasol while the committee bicycled alongside,
sometimes two to a bike, and here I came in triumph like
Britannia in a carnival float representing Empire, or,
depending on how you look at it, the Oppression of the
Indian People, which is how you *will* look at it and no
doubt you're right but I never saw anyone less oppressed
than Mr Coomaraswami, whose entire twenty stone shakes
with laughter all the time. The Hot Weather, they tell me,
is about to start, but I can't imagine anything hotter than
this, and it will be followed by the Wet Season, though I
already feel as though I am sitting in a puddle. Everything
which requires movement must be accomplished between
sunrise and breakfast, by which time inside is too hot to
move and outside is too hot to think. My bedroom, apart
from the ceiling fan, also has a punkah, which is like a line
of washing worked by a punkah-wallah who sits outside
and flaps the thing by a system of ropes and pulleys – or
would if he were ever here, which he isn't. At sundown,
gentle movement may be contemplated, and on Mondy I
was brought forth to deliver my lecture to a packed house,
Mr C's house, in fact, and a much more sensible house
than mine – built round a square courtyard, with a flat roof
all around so I had an audience in the gods like gods in the
audience, and though I say it myself I did a good one,
encouraged by the sight of several copies of *Venus* and
Nymph, in the front rows, and it all went terribly well
except for a nasty moment when questions were invited and
the very first one went – '

QUESTIONER: Miss Crewe, it is said you are an intimate friend of Mr H. G. Wells –

FLORA: ' – and I thought, God, how unfair! – to have come all this way to be gossiped about as if one were still in the Queen's Elm – '

PIKE: A public house in the Fulham area of Chelsea.

FLORA: ' – but it turned out nothing was meant by it except – '

QUESTIONER: Does Mr Wells write his famous books with a typewriter or with pen and ink?

FLORA: (*Firmly*) With pen and ink, a Waterman fountain pen, a present from his wife.
'Not that I had the least idea – Herbert did damn little writing when I was around, and made sure I did even less.'

PIKE: FC's liaison with Wells began no earlier than November 1929 and was therefore short, possibly the weekend of December 7th and 8th.

FLORA: 'After which there was a reception with lemonade and whisky and delicious snacks and conversation – darling, it's so moving, they read the *New Statesman* and *Time and Tide* and the *TLS* as if they were the Bible in parts (well, I don't mean the *Bible* but you know what I mean) and they know who wrote what about whom; it's like children with their faces jammed to the railings of an unattainable park. They say to me – '

QUESTIONER: What is your opinion of Gertrude Stein, Miss Crewe?

FLORA: ' – and I can't bring myself to say she's a poisonous old baggage who's travelling on a platform ticket – '

PIKE: FC's animosity towards Gertrude Stein should not lend credence to Hemingway's fanciful assertion (in a letter to Marlene Dietrich) that Stein threatened to scratch FC's or (the possessive pronoun is ambiguous) Alice Toklas's eyes out. If FC over-praised the chocolate cake, it would have been only out of politeness. (See 'Bunfight at 27 Rue de Fleurus' by E.C. Pike, Maryland Monographs, UMP, 1983).

FLORA: ' – but anyway that's when I met my artist.'

DAS: Miss Crewe, may I congratulate you on your lecture. I found it most interesting!

FLORA: Thank you . . . !

DAS: I was surprised you did not mention Virginia Woolf.

FLORA: I seldom do.

DAS: Have you met George Bernard Shaw?

FLORA: Yes. I was nearly in one of his plays once.

DAS: But are you not an actress . . . ?

FLORA: No, that was the trouble.

DAS: What do you think of Jummapur?

FLORA: Well, I only arrived on Saturday but –

DAS: Of course. How absurd of me!

FLORA: Not at all. I was going to say that my first impressions –

DAS: Jummpur is not in any case to be compared with London. Do you live in Bloomsbury?

FLORA: No, I live in Chelsea.

DAS: Chelsea – of course! My favourite part of London!

FLORA: Oh! you . . . ?

DAS: I hope to visit London one of these days. The Chelsea of Turner and the Pre-Raphaelite Brotherhood! Rossetti lived in Cheen Walk! Holman Hunt lived in Old Church Street! 'The Hireling Shepherd' was *painted* in Old Church Street! What an inspiration it would be to me to visit Chelsea!

FLORA: You are a painter!

DAS: Yes! Nirad Das.

FLORA: How do you do?

DAS: I am top hole. Thank you. May I give you a present?

FLORA: Oh . . .

DAS: Please do not judge it too harshly, Miss Crewe . . .

FLORA: But it's wonderful. Thank you.

' – and he gave me a pencil sketch of myself holding forth on the literary life, and the next thing I knew I'd agreed to sit for him. He is charming and eager and looks like a rosewood Charlie Chaplin, not the jumpy one in the films, the real one who was at Iris's tennis party.'

PIKE: Iris Tree was the daughter of Sir Herbert Beerbohm Tree, who, soon after the Crewe family arrived in London, gave FC her first employment, fleetingly as a cockney bystander in the original production of *Pygmalion*, and, after objections from Mrs Patrick Campbell, more permanently 'in the office'. It was this connection which brought FC into the orbit of Iris and her friend Nancy Cunard, and thence to the Sitwells, and arguably to the writing of poetry. FC's first poems, written in 1914–15, now lost, were submitted to the Sitwell magazine *Wheels*, and although they were not accepted (how they could have been worse than Miss Tree's contributions to *Wheels* is difficult to imagine), FC remained to become a loyal footsoldier in the Sitwells' war against 'the Enemy'.

FLORA: 'He is rather virile in a compact sort of way, with curly hair and hot brown eyes; he smiles a lot, he's got the teeth for it, white as his pyjamas.'

(DAS, *painting, is heard grunting in exasperation.*)

'Not that he's smiling at the moment. When I glance up I can see him frowning at me and then at the canvas as if one of us had misbehaved. By the way, I don't mean I've seen him in his pyjamas, darling, it's what he goes about in. At the Theosophical there was everything from loincloths like Gandhi to collars and ties. Which reminds me, I had a visit from a clean young Englishman who has asked me to dinner tonight at the Brits' Club. It was a bit of an afterthought really. I think I made a gaffe by not announcing myself to the Resident, the Senior Brit, and the young man, he was on a horse, was sent to look me over. I think he ticked me off but he was so nice it was hard to tell.'

(DAS *is heard sighing.*)

'I've a feeling I'm going to have to stop in a minute. My poem, the one I'm not writing, is about sitting still and being hot. It got defeated by its subject matter. Ask Dr Guppy – '

PIKE: Dr Alfred Guppy had been the Crewe family doctor since the move from Ashbourne to London in 1913. His notes on FC's illness, with references to pulmonary congestion, are first dated 1926.

FLORA: ' – if this is what he meant by a warm climate.'

33

DAS: Oh, fiddlesticks!

FLORA: I'm sorry. Is it my fault?

DAS: No, how can it be?

FLORA: Is that so silly?

DAS: No . . . forgive me! Oh dear, Miss Crewe! Yesterday I felt
. . . a communion and today –

FLORA: Oh! It *is* my fault! Yesterday I was writing a poem, and
today I have been writing a letter. That's what it is.

DAS: A letter?

FLORA: I am not the same sitter. How thoughtless of me. How
could I expect to be the same writing to my sister as for
writing my poem.

DAS: Yes. Yes.

FLORA: Are you angry?

DAS: I don't know. Can we stop now? I would like a cigarette.
Would you care for a cigarette? They are Goldflake.

FLORA: No. But I'd like you to smoke.

DAS: Thank you. You were writing to your sister? She is in
England, of course.

FLORA: Yes. Her name is Eleanor. She is much younger than
me; only twenty-three.

DAS: Then she cannot be so much younger.

FLORA: Routine gallantry is disappointing in a man.

DAS: I'm sorry.

FLORA: I am thirty-five and I look well enough on it.

DAS: I guessed your age to be thirty-two, if it is all right to say
so.

FLORA: Yes, it is all right to say so.

DAS: Where does your sister live?

FLORA: That's almost the first thing you asked *me*. Would it
mean anything to you?

(DAS *is loosening up again, regaining his normal good nature.*)

DAS: Oh, I have the whole of London spread out in my
imagination. Challenge me, you will see!

FLORA: All right, she lives in Holborn.

DAS: (*Pause*) Oh. Which part of London is that?

FLORA: Well, it's – oh dear – between the Gray's Inn Road
and –

DAS: Holl-born!

FLORA: Yes. Holborn.

DAS: But of course I know Holl-born! Charles Dickens lived in Doughty Street.

FLORA: Yes. Eleanor lives in Doughty Street.

DAS: But, Miss Crewe, *Oliver Twist* was written in that very street!

FLORA: Well, that's where Eleanor lives, near her work. She is the secretary to the editor of a weekly, the *Flag*.

DAS: The *Flag*!

FLORA: You surely have never read that too?

DAS: No, but I have met the editor of the *Flag* –

FLORA: (*Realizing*) Yes, of course you have! That is how I came to be here. Mr Chamberlain gave me letters of introduction.

DAS: His lecture in Jummapur caused the Theosophical Society to be suspended for one year.

FLORA: I'm sorry. But it's not for me to apologize for the Raj.

DAS: Oh, it was not the Raj but the Rajah! His Highness is our only capitalist! Do you agree with Mr Chamberlain's theory of Empire? I was not persuaded. Of course I am not an economist.

FLORA: That wouldn't deter Mr Chamberlain.

DAS: It is not my impression that England's imperial adventure is simply to buy time against revolution at home.

FLORA: I try to keep an open mind. Political theories are often, and perhaps entirely, a function of temperament. Eleanor and Mr Chamberlain are well suited.

DAS: Your sister shares Mr Chamberlain's opinions?

FLORA: Naturally. For reasons I have implied.

DAS: Yes. Being his secretary, you mean.

FLORA: Being his mistress.

DAS: Oh.

FLORA: You should have been a barrister, Mr Das.

DAS: I am justly rebuked!

FLORA: It was not a rebuke. An unintended slight, perhaps.

DAS: I am very sorry about your sister. It must be a great sadness for you.

35

FLORA: I am very happy for her.

DAS: But she will never be married now! Unless Mr Chamberlain marries her.

FLORA: He is already married, otherwise he might.

DAS: Oh my goodness. How different things are. Here, you see, your sister would have been cast out – for bringing shame on her father's house.

(FLORA *chuckles and he becomes angry.*)

Yes, perhaps we are not so enlightened as you.

FLORA: I'm sorry. I was only laughing because the difference is not the one you think. My father cast Eleanor out but the shame for him was Mr Chamberlain's politics. Poor father. A poet and a Communist . . . he must have felt like King Lear. Well, you have had your cigarette. Are we going to continue?

DAS: No, not today.

FLORA: I'll go back to my poem.

DAS: I have an appointment I had forgotten.

FLORA: Oh.

DAS: Actually you mustn't feel obliged . . . (DAS *is heard gathering together his paraphernalia, apparently in a hurry now.*)

FLORA: What have I done?

DAS: Done? What should you have done?

FLORA: Stop it. Please. Stop being Indian. (*Pause.*) Oh, I understand. (*Pause.*) Yes, yes. I did look.

DAS: Yes.

FLORA: I had a peep. Why not? You wanted me to.

DAS: Yes, why not? You looked at the painting and you decided to spend the time writing letters. Why not?

FLORA: I'm sorry.

DAS: You still have said nothing about the painting.

FLORA: I know.

DAS: I cannot continue today.

FLORA: I understand. Will we try again tomorrow?

DAS: Tomorrow is Sunday.

FLORA: The next day.

DAS: Perhaps I cannot continue at all.

FLORA: Oh. And all because I said nothing. Are you at the mercy of every breeze that blows? Or fails to blow? Are you an artist at all?

DAS: Perhaps not! A mere sketcher – a hack painter who should be working in the bazaar!

FLORA: Stop it.

DAS: Or in chalks on the ghat.

FLORA: Stop! I'm ashamed of you. And don't cry.

DAS: I will if I wish. Excuse me. I cannot manage the easel on my bicycle. I will send for it.
(*It becomes a physical tussle, a struggle. She begins to gasp as she speaks.*)

FLORA: You will not! And you will not take your box either. Give it to me – put it back –

DAS: I do not want to continue, Miss Crewe. Please let go!

FLORA: I *won't* let you give in –

DAS: Let go, damn you, someone will see us!
(FLORA *falls over, gasping for breath.*)
Oh . . . oh, Miss Crewe – oh, my God – let me help you. I'm sorry. Please. Here, sit down –
(*She has had an attack of breathlessness. He is helping her to a chair.* FLORA *speaks with difficulty.*)

FLORA: (*Her voice coming back*) Really, I'm all right. (*Pause.*) There.

DAS: What happened?

FLORA: I'm not allowed to wrestle with people. It's a considerable loss. My lungs are bad, you see.

DAS: Let me move the cushion.

FLORA: It's all right. I'm back now. Panic over. I'm here for my health, you see. Well, not *here* . . . I'll stay longer in the Hills.

DAS: Yes, that will be better. You must go high.

FLORA: Yes. In a day or two.

DAS: What is the matter with you?

FLORA: Oh, sloshing about inside. Can't breath under water. I'm sorry if I frightened you.

DAS: You did frighten me. Would you allow me to remain a little while?

FLORA: Yes. I would like you to. I'm soaking.

DAS: You must change your clothes.

FLORA: Yes. I'll go in now. I've got a shiver. Pull me up. Thank you. Ugh. I need to be rubbed down like a horse.

DAS: Perhaps some tea . . . I'll go to the kitchen and tell –

FLORA: Yes. Would you? I'll have a shower and get into my Wendy House.

DAS: Your . . . ?

FLORA: My mosquito net. I love my mosquito net. My big towel is on the kitchen verandah – would you ask Nazrul to put it in the bedroom?

(DAS *is shouting for* NAZRUL *in the inner part of the house. The action stays with* FLORA *as she goes into the interior, undressing, and through a door. She turns a squeaky tap. There is no sound of water, only a thumping in the pipes.*)

Oh, damn, come on, damn you.

DAS: (*Off*) Miss Crewe! I'm sorry, there's –

FLORA: Yes, no water.

DAS: (*Off*) It's the electricity for the pump.

FLORA: Yes. (*She turns the tap again. The thumping in the pipes ceases.*) I have to lie down. (*She moves.*) There's water in the pitcher, on the washstand.

DAS: Nazrul is not – oh! Oh, I'm so sorry! –

FLORA: I'm sorry, Mr Das, but really I feel too peculiar to mind at the moment.

DAS: Please take the towel.

FLORA: Thank you. No, please, get the water jug and my face cloth from the wash-stand.

(*He moves; he lifts the jug.*)

Is there any water?

DAS: Yes, it's full . . . Here –

FLORA: Thank you. Hold the towel. (*She pours a little water over herself.*) Oh, heaven. Would you pour it – over my back, not too much at a time. Oh, thank you. I'm terribly sorry about this. And my head. Oh, that's good. I feel as weak as a kitten. (*The water splashes down over her and on to the floor.*)

DAS: I'm afraid that's all.

FLORA: Thank you.

DAS: Here . . . should I dry you?

FLORA: My back please. Rub hard. Thank you. (*Her voice comes out shivery.*) Thank you. Stop a minute.
(*She takes the towel. She uses it and gives it back to* DAS.)
There. Thank you. And my legs. Thank you.

DAS: There was no one in the kitchen. And no water for tea.

FLORA: Never mind. I'll get into bed now. (*She does so. She has to draw the net aside.*)

DAS: Do you have soda water?

FLORA: I think so.

DAS: I will fetch it.

FLORA: Yes please. In the fridge.

DAS: Yes. Oh, but is it locked?

FLORA: Oh . . . perhaps. Now I'm hot again, and no electricity for the fan. The sheet's too hot. It's too late for modesty. Anyway, I'm your model.

DAS: I will fetch soda water.

FLORA: That was the thing I was going to ask you.

DAS: When?

FLORA: The delicate question . . . whether you would prefer to paint me nude.

DAS: Oh.

FLORA: I preferred it. I had more what-do-you-call-it.

DAS: *Rasa*.

FLORA: (*Laughs quietly*) Yes, *rasa*.

MRS SWAN: I remember the frock. It was not quite such a royal blue. Her cornflower dress, she called it.

ANISH: And her? Is it a good likeness?

MRS SWAN: Well, it's certainly Flora. She always sat upright and square to the table; she hated slouchers. She would have made a good schoolmistress, except for the feet. She always slipped her shoes off to work, and placed them neatly to one side like that. Yes, it's a very faithful portrait.

ANISH: But unfinished.

MRS SWAN: Is it? Why do you say that?

ANISH: It wasn't clear from the book, the way they cropped the painting. See here, my father has only indicated the tree – and the monkey – especially the doorway beyond . . .

MRS SWAN: Oh, but it's a portrait of *her*.

ANISH: Yes but he wasn't satisfied with her. He would have gone back to complete the background only when he considered the figure finished. Believe me. My father abandoned this portrait. I wondered why he hadn't signed it. Now I know. Thank you for showing it to me.

MRS SWAN: Mr Das, you said you had come to show *me* something. *Evidence* you said –

ANISH: Yes! I did. Come into the hall, Mrs Swan. Can you guess what it is?

MRS SWAN: A photograph of your father looking like Charlie Chaplin.

ANISH: (*Off*) No, better evidence than that. You may be shocked.

MRS SWAN: (*Approaching*) Oh dear, then you had better prepare me.

ANISH: It's a painting of course . . . wrapped up in this paper for sixty years.
(*He unwraps the paper.*) We need a flat surface, in the light –

MRS SWAN: The table in the bay . . .

ANISH: Yes, please come to the window –
>   (*They are moving, she with her stick.*)
>   May I use the elephants? To hold it flat.
MRS SWAN: Very suitable.
ANISH: And there you are, then.
MRS SWAN: (*Taken aback*) Oh, good heavens.
ANISH: A second portrait of Flora Crewe.
MRS SWAN: Oh . . . How like Flora.
ANISH: More than a good likeness, Mrs Swan.
MRS SWAN: No . . . I mean *how like Flora*!

DAS: (*Approaching*) Nazrul has returned, most fortunately. I was able to unlock the refrigerator. I have the soda water.

FLORA: Thank you. You must have some too.

DAS: I will put it on the table.

FLORA: Yes. No – no, the table by me. It's quite safe, I've covered myself.

DAS: May I move this book?

FLORA: Thank you. Do you know it? I found it here.

DAS: *Up the Country* . . . No. It looks old.

FLORA: A hundred years before my time, but it's just my book.

DAS: Oh – let me – let me pour the water for you.

FLORA: Thank you.

DAS: (*While pouring water from the bottle into a glass*) Nazrul was delayed at the shops by a riot, he says. The police charged the mob with lathis, he could have easily been killed, but by heroism and inspired by his loyalty to the memsahib he managed to return only an hour late with all the food you gave him money for except two chickens which were torn from his grasp.

FLORA: Oh dear . . . you thanked him, I hope.

DAS: I struck him, of course. You should fine him for the chickens.

FLORA: (*Drinking*) Oh, that's nice. It's still cold. Perhaps there really was a riot.

DAS: Oh, yes. Very probably. I have sent Nazrul to fetch the dhobi – you must have fresh linen for the bed. Nazrul will bring water but you must not drink it.

FLORA: Thank you.

(*The noise of the punkah begins quietly.*)

DAS: I'm sure the electricity will return soon and the fan will be working.

FLORA: What's that? Oh, the punkah!

DAS: I have found a boy to be punkah-wallah.

FLORA: Yes, it makes a draught. Thank you. A *little* boy?

42

DAS: Don't worry about him. I've told him the memsahib is sick.

FLORA: The memsahib. Oh dear.

DAS: Yes, you are memsahib. Are you all right now, Miss Crewe?

FLORA: Oh yes. I'm only shamming now.

DAS: May I return later to make certain?

FLORA: Are you leaving now? Yes, I've made you late.

DAS: No, not at all. There is no one waiting for me. But the servants will return and . . . we Indians are frightful gossips, you see.

FLORA: Oh.

DAS: It is for yourself, not me.

FLORA: I don't believe you, Mr Das, not entirely.

DAS: To tell you the truth, this is the first time I have been alone in a room with an Englishwoman.

FLORA: Oh. Well, you certainly started at the deep end.

DAS: We need not refer to it again. It was an accident.

FLORA: I didn't think you blushed.

DAS: (*Coldly*) Oh, yes. I assure you our physiology is exactly the same as yours.

FLORA: Well said, but I didn't mean that. I was being personal. I didn't expect an artist to blush.

DAS: Then perhaps I am not an artist, as you said.

FLORA: I did not. All I did was hold my tongue and you wanted to cut and run. What would you have done in the ordinary rough and tumble of literary life in London – on which, as you know, I am an expert. I give lectures on it. I expect you would have hanged yourself by now. When *Nymph In Her Orisons* came out one of the reviewers called it *Nymph In Her Mania*, and made some play with 'free verse' and 'free love', as if my poems, which I had found so hard to write, were a kind of dalliance, no more than that. *I* cried a bit too. *I* wanted to cut and run. Oh, the dreadful authority of print. It's bogus. If free verse and free love have anything in common it's a distrust of promiscuity. Quite apart from it not applying to me . . .

DAS: Of course not!

FLORA: Bogus and ignorant. My poems are not free verse.

DAS: Oh . . .

FLORA: I met my critic somewhere a few months later and poured his drink over his head and went home and wrote a poem. So that was all right. But he'd taken weeks away from me and I mind that now.

DAS: Oh! You're not dying are you?

FLORA: I expect so, but I intend to take years and years about it. You'll be dead too, one day, so let it be a lesson to you. Ignore everything, including silence. I was silent about your painting, if you want to know, because I thought you'd be an *Indian* artist.

DAS: An Indian artist?

FLORA: Yes. You *are* an Indian artist, aren't you? Stick up for yourself. Why do you like everything English?

DAS: I do not like everything English.

FLORA: Yes, you do. You're enthralled. Chelsea, Bloomsbury, *Oliver Twist*, Goldflake cigarettes . . . even painting in oils, that's not Indian. You're trying to paint me from my point of view instead of yours – what you *think* is my point of view. You *deserve* the bloody Empire!

DAS: (*Sharply*) May I sit down, please?

FLORA: Yes, do. Flora is herself again.

DAS: I will move the chair near the door.

FLORA: You can move the chair on to the verandah if you like, so the servants won't –

DAS: I would like to smoke, that is what I meant.

FLORA: Oh. I'm sorry. Thank you. In that case, can you see me through the net from over there?

DAS: Barely.

FLORA: Is that no or yes? Oof! That's better! That's what I love about my little house – you can see out but you can't see in.

DAS: (*Passionately*) But you are looking out at such a house! The bloody Empire finished off Indian painting! (*Pause.*) Excuse me.

FLORA: No, I prefer your bark.

DAS: Perhaps your sister is right. And Mr Chamberlain. Perhaps we have been robbed. Yes; when the books are balanced.

The women here wear saris made in Lancashire. The
cotton is Indian but we cannot compete in the weaving. Mr
Chamberlain explained it all to us in simple Marxist
language. Actually, he caused some offence.

FLORA: Yes, you mean the Rajah . . .

DAS: No, no – he didn't realize we had Marxists of our own,
many of them in the Jummapur Theosophical Society. For
some, Marx is the god whose wisdom the Society honours
in its title!

FLORA: Mr Coomaraswami . . . ?

DAS: No, not Mr Coomaraswami. *His* criticism is that you
haven't exploited India *enough*. 'Where are the cotton mills?
The steel mills? No investment, no planning. The Empire
has failed us!' That is Mr Coomaraswami. Well, the
Empire will one day be gone, like the Mughal Empire
before it, and only their monuments remain – the visions of
Shah Jahan! – of Sir Edwin Lutyens!

FLORA: 'Look on my works, ye mighty, and despair!'

DAS: (*Delighted*) Oh, yes! Finally like the empire of
Ozymandias! Entirely forgotten except in a poem by an
English poet. You see how privileged we are, Miss Crewe.
Only in art can empires cheat oblivion, because only the
artist can say, 'Look on my works, ye mighty, and despair!'

FLORA: Well, it helps if he happens to be Shelley.

DAS: There are Mughal paintings in the museum in London.

FLORA: Yes. Rajput miniatures in the Victoria and Albert.

DAS: You have seen them?

FLORA: Yes.

DAS: And you like them, of course.

FLORA: Yes. Very much.

DAS: Eighteenth and early nineteenth century, or earlier,
nothing much good later.

FLORA: I didn't mean I expected you to paint like that. I just
didn't like you thinking English was better because it was
English. If that is what you were thinking.
Did you consider my question?

DAS: What question?

FLORA: Can't you paint me without thinking of Rossetti or

Millais? Especially without thinking of Holman Hunt.
Would your nudes be Pre-Raphaelite too?

DAS: The Pre-Raphaelites did not paint nudes. Their models
were clothed.

FLORA: Oh, yes, weren't they though! The Brotherhood painted
life as if it were a costume drama put on by Beerbohm
Tree. I knew him, you know. He gave me my first job.
And my second. All right, Alma-Tadema, then. I bet you
like Alma-Tadema.

DAS: Yes, very much. When you stood . . . with the pitcher of
water, you were an Alma-Tadema.

FLORA: Well, I don't want to be painted like that either – that's
C. B. Cochran, if only he dared.

DAS: I don't understand why you are angry with me.

FLORA: You were painting me as a gift, to please me.

DAS: Yes. Yes, it was a gift for you.

FLORA: If you don't start learning to *take* you'll never be shot of
us. Who whom? Nothing else counts. Mr Chamberlain is
bosh. Mr Coomaraswami is bosh. It's your country, and
we've got it. Everything else is bosh. When I was Modi's
model I might as well have *been* a table. 'Lie down – thrust
your hips.' When he was satisfied, he got rid of me. There
was no question who whom. You'd never change his colour
on a map. But please light your Goldflake.

(*Pause.* DAS *lights his cigarette with a match.*)

DAS: I like the Pre-Raphaelites because they tell stories. That is
my tradition too. I am Rajasthani. Our art is narrative art,
stories from the legends and romances. The English
painters had the Bible and Shakespeare, King Arthur . . .
We had the Bhagavata Purana, and the Rasikpriya, which
was written exactly when Shakespeare had his first play.
And long before Chaucer we had the Chaurapanchasika,
from Kashmir, which is poems of love written by the poet
of the court on his way to his execution for falling in love
with the king's daugher, and the king liked the poems so
very much he pardoned the poet and allowed the lovers to
marry.

FLORA: Oh . . .

DAS: But the favourite book of the Rajput painters was the Gita
      Govinda, which tells the story of Krishna and Radha, the
      most beautiful of the herdswomen.
      (*The ceiling-fan starts working.*)
FLORA: The fan has started. The electricity is on.
DAS: You will be a little cooler now.
FLORA: Yes. I might have a sleep.
DAS: That would be good.
FLORA: Mr Durance has invited me to dinner at the Club.
DAS: Will you be well enough?
FLORA: I am well now.
DAS: That is good. Goodbye, then.
FLORA: Were Krishna and Radha punished in the story?
DAS: What for?
FLORA: I should have come here years ago. The punkah boy can
      stop now. Will you give him a rupee? I'll return it
      tomorrow.
DAS: I will give him an anna. A rupee would upset the market.

ANISH: I was in England when my father died. It was Christmas day, 1967. My first Christmas in London, in a house of student bedsits in Ladbroke Grove. An unhappy day.

MRS SWAN: Yes, of course.

ANISH: I mean it was already unhappy. The house was cold and empty. All the other students had gone home to their families, naturally. I was the only one left. No one had invited me.

MRS SWAN: Well, having a Hindu for Christmas can be tricky. Francis would invite his Assistant for Christmas lunch, and I always felt I should be apologizing for rubbing something in which left him out, if you follow me. It quite spoiled the business of the paper hats too. There's nothing like having an Indian at table for making one feel like a complete ass handing round the vegetables in a pink paper fez. That was after I-zation, of course.

ANISH: I heard the telephone . . .

MRS SWAN: Did you? Well, it's stopped now. The mistletoe was another problem.

ANISH: . . . no, there was a coin box in the hall. I could hear it ringing all day. It would stop and then start again. I ignored it. The phone was never for me. But finally I went up and answered it, and it was my uncle calling from Jummapur to say my father was dead.

MRS SWAN: Oh, how sad. Did you go home?

ANISH: Yes. There was great sadness in our house.

MRS SWAN: Of course . . .

ANISH: I'm ashamed of it but I found the rituals of death and grief distasteful. I wanted to return to England. And I did, as soon as permitted. There were legal matters which I was grateful to leave to my father's elder brother. So I was in England again when I learned that I had a legacy from my father. He had left me his tin trunk which had always stood at the foot of his bed.

48

MRS SWAN: Ah, yes . . .

ANISH: It arrived finally and it was locked. There had been no mention of a key. So I broke the hasp. There was nothing of value in the trunk that I could see.

MRS SWAN: You were disappointed?

ANISH: Well, yes. It was mainly letters and old bills, my report cards from school, and so on. But at the bottom of everything was a painting rolled up in paper. An extraordinary painting, a nude, a portrait of a woman. Even more amazing, a European woman, apparently painted many years before. I couldn't imagine who she was or what it meant.

MRS SWAN: Did you ask anyone? Your uncle?

ANISH: No. It was clear that this was something my father was sharing with me alone. A secret he was passing on. So I rolled the picture up again and put it away. I never hung it, of course. I never showed it to anyone, until years later I showed it to my wife.

MRS SWAN: Until now.

ANISH: Yes, until a week ago. The book in the shop window. It was like seeing a ghost. Not her ghost; his. It was my father's hand – his work – I had grown up watching him work, his portrait-work, in oils – local bigwigs, daughters of well-to-do businessmen. I had seen a hundred original Nirad Dases, and here was his work, not once but repeated twenty times over. It filled the window of the bookshop, a special display . . . *The Selected Letters of Flora Crewe*, and in the next instant I saw it was the same woman.

MRS SWAN: Yes. Oh, yes, it's Flora. It's as particular as an English miniature. A watercolour, isn't it?

ANISH: Watercolour and gouache, on paper.

MRS SWAN: It's fascinating. It looks Indian but he hasn't made *her* Indian.

ANISH: Well, she was *not* Indian.

MRS SWAN: Yes, I know. I'm not gaga, I'm only old. I mean he hasn't painted her flat. But everything else looks Indian, like enamel . . . the moon and stars done with a pastry cutter. And the birds singing in the border. Or is that the ceiling of the room, that line?

ANISH: I'm not sure.

MRS SWAN: And the foliage in bloom, so bright. Is it day or night? I know what's odd. The different parts are on different scales. The tree is far too small, or it's the right size too close. You can't tell if the painter is in the house or outside looking in.

ANISH: She is in a house within a house . . . look.

MRS SWAN: This edge must be the floor. Flora wrote about animals scratching about under the bungalow. There's a snake, look. Oh, but there couldn't have been gazelles under the house, could there? Perhaps it's a border after all . . . or a touch of fancy.

ANISH: Symbolism, yes.

MRS SWAN: I like the book on the pillow. That's Flora.

ANISH: And a pitcher on the table next to her, and bread on the plate . . . Do you see the lettering on the book?

MRS SWAN: Too small. I could find a magnifying glass . . .

ANISH: It says 'Eden'.

MRS SWAN: Eden? . . . (*Understanding.*) Oh!

ANISH: A book of verses underneath the bough, a jug of wine, a loaf of bread and thou beside me singing in the wilderness!

MRS SWAN: That's not Indian.

ANISH: No. The Mughals brought miniature painting from Persia when they made their Indian empire. But Muslim and Hindu art are different. The Muslim artists were realists. To a Hindu every object has an inner meaning, everything is to be interpreted in a language of symbols –

MRS SWAN: Which you understand, Mr Das?

ANISH: Not in detail. I'd have to look it up.

MRS SWAN: (*Amused*) Look it up! (*Apologizing.*) Oh, I'm sorry.

ANISH: But this flowering vine that winds itself around the dark trunk of the tree . . .

MRS SWAN: Oh . . .

ANISH: The vine is shedding its leaves and petals, look where they're falling to the ground. I think my father knew your sister was dying.

MRS SWAN: It upsets me, to see her nakedness.

ANISH: Yes . . . it's unguarded; she is not posing but resting –

MRS SWAN: No, I did not mean that. I don't make presumptions.

ANISH: Oh . . . but . . .

MRS SWAN: I was not there to nurse her . . . bathe her . . . I never saw her body at the end.

ANISH: Yes. Let me put it away now.

MRS SWAN: No, leave it, please. I want to look at it more. Yes. Such a pretty painting.

ANISH: It was done with great love.

MRS SWAN: He was certainly taken with her. Whether she posed for him, or whether it's a work of the imagination . . .

ANISH: Oh . . . but the symbolism clearly –

MRS SWAN: Codswallop. Your 'house within a house', as anyone can see, is a mosquito net. I had one which was gathered at the top in exactly that way. And a drink and a sandwich don't add up to the *Rubáiyát of Omar Khayyám* by a long chalk. Eden, indeed! Why would a Hindu call it Eden?

ANISH: *Her* paradise, not his –

MRS SWAN: Don't be a fool. The book is a volume of Indian travels. It was Flora's bedside reading. She mentions it in one of her letters – you should read the footnotes.

FLORA: 'Jummapur. Sunday. April 6th. Darling Nell, I posted a
letter only hours ago – at least I put it in the box at the
Club last night and no doubt it's still there – but I'll make
this the next page of my journal and probably post it when
I leave Jummapur. We had an excitement in town
yesterday morning, a riot, and half a street of shops burned
to the ground, with the police out in force – the Rajah's
police. The Rajah of Jummapur is Hindu (otherwise it
would more likely be Jumma*bad* – not – *pur*) but the
Muslims got the best of it according to my cook, who was
in the heat of the battle. The Brits here shake their heads
and ask where will it all end when we've gone, because
going we are. That's official. Tell Josh. I got it from the
Resident, whose view is that (a) it is our moral duty to
remain and (b) we will shirk it. So now it's Sunday after
breakfast, and I've been horse riding! – in a long skirt like
the Viceroy's daughters twenty years ago, the first women
to ride astride in India. Do you remember Llandudno? No,
you surely can't. I think that was the last time I was ever
on anything resembling a horse.'

PIKE: The Crewe family spent August at the seaside resort in
North Wales from 1904 until 1911, the year of Mrs Crewe's
elopement. FC's allusion is evidently to donkey rides on
the sands, and her comment is of some interest, since, if
she is right, a recently published photograph described as
showing FC and Maynard Keynes on horseback at
Garsington in 1924 (*Ottoline Morrell and Her Circle in Hell*,
by Toshiro Kurasaki, 1988) misidentifies her; if not him.

FLORA: 'If I start coming over a bit dated it's because in my
bungalow, which is not duck but dak, i.e. for travellers (as
Josh has probably told you by now), I have discovered
among a box of dilapidated railway novels a book of letters
written from India a hundred years ago by an English

spinster – hand on my heart – to her sister Eleanor in
London, and this is now my only reading.'

PIKE: The spinster was Emily Eden and the book was *Up the
Country*, 1866. The Hon. Miss Eden was accompanying her
brother, the Governor-General Lord Auckland, on an
official progress up country. The tour, supported by a
caravan of ten thousand people, including Auckland's
French chef, and almost as many animals, lasted thirty
months, from October 1837, and Emily wrote hundreds of
letters to sisters and friends at home, happily unaware that
the expedition's diplomatic and strategic accomplishment
was to set the stage for the greatest military disaster ever to
befall the British under arms, the destruction of the army
in Afghanistan.

FLORA: 'I shall steal the book when I leave here in a day or two
and pick up Emily's trail in Delhi and Simla and up into
the Punjab, where the literary societies are holding their
breath. Speaking of which, I am doing pretty well with
mine, well enough to go dancing last night. My suitor (I
suppose I must call him that, though I swear I did nothing
to encourage him) came to fetch me in an enormous open
Daimler which drew a crowd.'

(*Sound of the Daimler and the crowd.*)

(*Calling out from off*) You wangled it!

(*Sounds of* DURANCE *opening the driver's door and closing it
again.* FLORA *has opened the passenger door, got into the car
and slammed the door. The ambience is the hubbub of Indian
voices, children, dogs, chickens . . . general excitement.*)
Can I drive?

DURANCE: Next time. Is that a bargain?

FLORA: It's a bargain.

DURANCE: Done. By the way, I hope you'll call me David. First
names are generally the drill with us.

FLORA: David.

(*Sounds of* DURANCE *shouting, in Urdu, to clear a path. The
car honks its horn and moves.*)
'And off we went, pushing through the mob of curiosity
seekers, scattering children and dogs and chickens right

and left, rather like leaving Bow Street in a police van. My God, how strange; that was ten years ago almost to the day.'

PIKE: In fact, nine. See 'The Woman Who Wrote What She Knew', by E. C. Pike (Maryland Monographs, UMP, 1981).

FLORA: 'I fully expected the Club to be like a commercial hotel in the hotter part of Guildford, but not at all – it's huge and white and pillared, just like the house of your first memory, perhaps – poor mama's nearly-house, which was ours for six months and then no more. I've never been back to Maybrook, perhaps we should make a pilgrimage one day.'

PIKE: The Crewe family met Sir George Dewe-Lovett of Maybrook Hall, Lancashire, on the promenade at Llandudno in August 1911. Catherine Crewe never returned to the house at Ashbourne. She eloped with Dewe-Lovett, a director of the White Star Shipping Line, and took her daughters, who were aged four and sixteen, to live at Maybrook. Percival Crewe proved to be unacrimonious and divorce proceedings were under way when the girls returned to Ashbourne to stay with their father for the Easter holidays of 1912, while their mother joined Dewe-Lovett at Southampton. The *Titanic* sailed on April 10th and FC never saw her mother or Maybrook again.

FLORA: 'And everyone at the Club was very friendly, going out of their way to explain that although they didn't go in much for poetry, they had nothing against it, so that was all right, and dinner was soup, boiled fish, lamb cutlets, sherry trifle and sardines on toast – eight of us at the Resident's table – '

WOMAN: Are you writing a poem about India, Flora?

FLORA: Trying to.

MAN: Kipling – there was a poet! 'And the dawn comes up like thunder on the road to Mandalay!'

WOMAN: I thought that was a *song*.

FLORA: 'The Resident was a different matter – '

RESIDENT: The only poet I *know* is Alfred Housman. I expect you've come across him.

FLORA: Of course!

RESIDENT: How is he nowadays?

FLORA: Oh – come *across* him –

RESIDENT: He hauled me through *Ars Amatoria* when I was up at Trinity –

FLORA: *The Art of Love?*

RESIDENT: When it comes to love, he said, you're either an Ovid man or a Virgil man. *Omnia vincit amor* – that's Virgil – 'Love wins every time, and we give way to love' – *et nos cedamus amori*. Housman was an Ovid man – *et mihi cedet amor* – 'Love gives way to me'.

FLORA: I'm a Virgil man.

RESIDENT: Are you? Well, you meet more people that way.

FLORA: ' – and his sources of information were impressive.'

RESIDENT: I believe you're here on doctor's orders.

FLORA: Why . . . yes . . . how . . . ?

RESIDENT: If there's anything you need or want, you tell David – right, David?

DURANCE: Yes, sir.

FLORA: Thank you. He's already promised me a go in the Daimler.

DURANCE: (*Embarrassed*) Oh . . .

RESIDENT: If you like cars, the Rajah has got about eighty-six of them – Rollses, the lot. With about ten miles on the clock. Collects them like stamps. Well, don't let me stop you enjoying yourselves.

DURANCE: Would you like to dance, Flora?

FLORA: 'And it turned out to be an easy evening to get through, which only goes to show, when in Rome, etc., and I wish I'd remembered that when I *was* in Rome.'

PIKE: FC was in Rome twice, in 1920 and 1926, en route to Capri in each case. It is unclear what she means here.

FLORA: 'Interrupted!'

(*The gramophone dance music, which has been in the background, becomes the dominant sound as* DURANCE *and* FLORA *begin to dance.*)

DURANCE: Do you mean you've come to India for your health?

FLORA: Is that amusing?

DURANCE: Well, it is rather. Have you seen the English
    cemetery?

FLORA: No.

DURANCE: I must take you there.

FLORA: Oh.

DURANCE: People here drop like flies – cholera, typhoid,
    malaria – men, women and children, here one day, gone
    the next. Are you sure the doctor said India? Perhaps he
    said Switzerland and you weren't paying attention.

FLORA: He didn't say India. He said a sea voyage and
    somewhere warm – but I wanted to come to India.

DURANCE: Then good for you. Live dangerously, why not?

FLORA: Oh – you're too energetic for me – slow down!

DURANCE: Well, I suppose this is somewhere warm. In a month
    you can't imagine it – but you'll be gone to the hills, so
    you'll be all right.

FLORA: Yes. Let's sit down.

DURANCE: Slow one coming up . . . ?

FLORA: No, I'm out of puff.

    (*They stop dancing.*)

DURANCE: Yes, of course. You're not really bad, are you,
    Flora?

FLORA: No, but I'd rather sit down. Do you think there might
    be more air outside?

DURANCE: On the verandah? Any air that's going. Should we
    take a peg with us?

    (*He calls to a* SERVANT.)

    Koi-hai! Thank you – two burra pegs.

SERVANT: Yes, sir.

FLORA: Lots of soda with mine, please.

    (*They move further away from the music, which has continued,
    and come to the exterior, which makes its own noise, crickets,
    insects, leaves . . .*)

DURANCE: There we are. Long-sleever? Good for putting the
    feet up.

FLORA: Yes – long-sleever. Thank you. How pretty the lanterns . . .

DURANCE: I hope you don't mind the moths.

FLORA: No, I like moths.

DURANCE: If they make a whining noise, kill them.

FLORA: It's a nice Club.

DURANCE: Yes, it's decent enough. There are not so many British here so we tend to mix more.

FLORA: With the Indians?

DURANCE: No. In India proper, I mean *our* India, there'd be two or three Clubs. The box-wallahs would have their own and the government people would stick together, you know how it is – and the Army . . .

FLORA: Mr Das called you Captain.

DURANCE: Yes, I'm Army. Seconded, of course. There are two of us Juniors – political agents we call ourselves when we're on tour round the states. Jummapur is not one of your twenty-one-gun salute states, you see – my Chief is in charge of half-a-dozen native states.

FLORA: In charge?

DURANCE: Oh yes.

FLORA: Is he Army? No – how silly –

DURANCE: He's ICS. The heaven-born. A Brahmin.

FLORA: Not seriously?

DURANCE: Yes, seriously. Oh no, not a Brahmin seriously. But it might come to that with I-zation.

(FLORA *is puzzled by the word.*)

Indianization. It's all over, you know. We have Indian officers in the Regiment now. My fellow Junior here is Indian, too, terribly nice chap – he's ICS, passed the exam, did his year at Cambridge, learned polo and knives-and-forks, and here he is, a pukka sahib in the Indian Civil Service.

FLORA: But he's not here.

DURANCE: At the Club? No, he can't come into the Club.

(*The* SERVANT *arrives.*)

Ah, here we are. Thank you . . .

(*The* SERVANT *leaves.*)

Cheers. Your health, Flora. I drink to your health for which you came. I wish you were staying longer. I mean, only for my sake, Flora.

FLORA: Yes, but I'm not. So that's that. Don't look hangdog. You might like me less and less as you got to know me.

DURANCE: Will you come riding in the morning?

FLORA: Seriously.

DURANCE: Yes, seriously. Will you?

FLORA: In the Daimler?

DURANCE: No. Say you will. We'll have to go inside in a minute if no one comes out.

FLORA: Why?

DURANCE: There's nothing to do here except gossip, you see. Everyone is agog about you. One of the wives claims . . . Were you in the papers at home? Some scandal about one of your books, something like that?

FLORA: I can see why you're nervous, being trapped out here with me – let's go in –

DURANCE: No – I'm sorry. Flora . . . ? Pax? Please.

FLORA: All right. Pax.

(*He kisses her, uninvited, tentatively.*)

DURANCE: Sealed with a kiss.

FLORA: No more. I mean it, David. Think of your career.

DURANCE: Are you really a scandalous woman?

FLORA: I was for a while. I was up in court, you know. Bow Street.

DURANCE: (*Alarmed*) Oh, not really?

FLORA: Almost really. I was a witness. The publisher was in the dock, but it was my poems – *Venus In Her Season*, my first book.

DURANCE: Oh, I say.

FLORA: The case was dismissed on a technicality, and the policemen were awfully sweet; they got me away through the crowd in a van. It was all most enjoyable actually, and it gave me an entrée to several writers I admired, most of whom, it turned out, were hoping it worked the other way round. My sister was asked to leave school. But that was mostly my own fault – the magistrate asked me why all the

58

poems seemed to be about sex, and I said, 'Write what you know' – just showing off, I was practically a virgin, but it got me so thoroughly into the newspapers my name rings a bell even with the wife of a bloody jute planter or something in the middle of Rajputana, damn, damn, damn. No, let's go inside.

DURANCE: Sit down, that's an order. How's your whisky?

FLORA: Excellent. All the better for being forbidden. My God, where did that moon come from?

DURANCE: Better. I love this country, don't you?

FLORA: Yes, I think I do. What's going to happen to it? The riot in town this morning . . . does that happen often?

DURANCE: Not here, no. The gaols are filling up in British India.

FLORA: Well, then.

DURANCE: It wasn't against us, it was Hindu and Muslim. Gandhi's salt march reached the sea today, did you hear? Our Congress Hindus closed their shops in sympathy, and the Muslims wouldn't join in, that's all it was about. The Indian National Congress is all very well, but to the Muslims, Congress means Gandhi . . . a Hindu party in all but name.

FLORA: Will Gandhi be arrested?

DURANCE: No, no. The salt tax is a lot of nonsense actually.

FLORA: Yes, it does seem hard in a country like this.

DURANCE: Not that sort of nonsense. It works out at about four annas a year. Most Indians didn't even know there *was* a salt tax.

FLORA: Well, they do now.

DURANCE: Yes. They do now. Would you like one more turn round the floor before they play the King?

FLORA: No, I'm tiring. (*She gets up.*) Will you finish my whisky? I'd like to go back to my little house.

DURANCE: Yes, of course. Would you mind saying goodnight to my Chief? It would go down well.

FLORA: I'd like to. The Brahmin.

DURANCE: Yes. The highest caste of Hindu, you see, and the ICS are the highest caste of Anglo-India. There's about twelve hundred ICS and they run the continent. That's three for every million Indians.

FLORA: Why do the Indians let them?

DURANCE: Why not? They're better at it.

FLORA: Are they?

DURANCE: Ask them.

FLORA: Who?

DURANCE: The natives. Ask them. We've pulled this country together. It's taken a hundred years with a hiccup or two but the place now works.

FLORA: That's what you love, then? What you created?

DURANCE: Oh no, it's India I love. I'll show you.

(*A sudden combination of animal noises are heard – buffalo snorting, horses whinnying, Flora crying out.* FLORA *and* DURANCE *on horseback.*)

DURANCE: Did he frighten you? He's big but harmless.

FLORA: Oh my!

DURANCE: We surprised him in his bath.

FLORA: He's immense! Thank you!

DURANCE: Me?

FLORA: He was *my* surprise really.

DURANCE: Oh yes. Just for you.

FLORA: I've never been given a buffalo before.

DURANCE: Look – sand grouse! (*He makes a noise to represent the firing of a shotgun, both barrels.*) A nice left and right!

FLORA: Don't shoot them, they're mine! (*Her interior voice comes in, 'inside' the scene itself.*)

'Where life began at the lake's edge,
water and mud convulsed,
reared itself and became shaped
into buffalo.
The beast stood dismayed,
smeared with birth, streaming
from his muzzle like an infant, celebrated
with lily flowers about his horns.
So he walked away to meet his death
among peacocks, parrots, antelopes.
We watched him go, taller than he,
mounted astride, superior beasts.'

DURANCE: Time to trot – sun's up.

FLORA: Oops – David – I'll have to tell you – stop! It's my first time on a horse, you see.

DURANCE: Yes, I could tell.

FLORA: (*Miffed*) Could you? Even walking? I felt so proud when we were walking.

DURANCE: No, no good, I'm afraid.

FLORA: Oh, damn you. I'm going to get off.

DURANCE: No, no, just sit. He's a chair. Breathe in. India smells wonderful, doesn't it?

FLORA: Out here it does.

DURANCE: You should smell chapattis cooking on a camel-dung fire out in the Thar Desert. Perfume!

FLORA: What were you doing out there?

DURANCE: Cooking chapattis on a camel-dung fire. (*Laughs.*) I'll tell you where it all went wrong with us and India. It was the Suez Canal. It let the women in.

FLORA: Oh!

DURANCE: Absolutely. When you had to sail round the Cape this was a man's country and we mucked in with the natives. The memsahibs put a stop to that. The memsahib won't muck in, won't even be alone in a room with an Indian.

FLORA: Oh . . .

DURANCE: Don't point your toes out. May I ask you a personal question?

FLORA: No.

DURANCE: All right.

FLORA: I wanted to ask *you* something. How did the Resident know I came to India for my health?

DURANCE: It's his business to know. Shoulders back. Reins too slack.

FLORA: But I didn't tell anybody.

DURANCE: Obviously you did.

FLORA: Only Mr Das.

DURANCE: Oh, well, say no more. Jolly friendly of you, of course, sharing a confidence, lemonade, all that, but they can't help themselves bragging about it, telling all they know.

FLORA: (*Furious*) Rubbish!

DURANCE: Well . . . I stand corrected.

FLORA: I'm sorry. I don't believe you, though.

DURANCE: Righto.

FLORA: I'm sorry. Pax.

DURANCE: Flora.

FLORA: No.

DURANCE: Would you marry me?

FLORA: No.

DURANCE: Would you think about it?

FLORA: No. Thank you.

DURANCE: Love at first sight, you see. Forgive me.

FLORA: Oh, David.

DURANCE: Knees together.

FLORA: 'Fraid so.

> (*She laughs without malice but unrestrainedly. He punishes her without malice by breaking his horse into a trot. Her horse follows, trotting.* FLORA *squealing with fright and laughing.*)

Inside the bungalow.

FLORA: 'Next day. Oh dear, guess what? You won't approve. Quite right. So I think it's time to go. Love 'em and leave 'em.'

PIKE: What, if anything, came of this is not known. The man was most probably the Junior Political Agent at the Residency, Captain David Arthur Durance, who took FC dancing and horse riding. He was killed in Malaya in 1942 during the Japanese advance on Singapore.

FLORA: 'I feel tons better, though. The juices are starting to flow again, as you can see from the enclosed.'

PIKE: 'Buffalo' and 'Pearl', included in *Indian Ink*, 1932.

FLORA: 'I'll keep sending you fair copies of anything I finish in case I get carried away by monsoons or tigers, and if I do, look after the comma after "astride", please, it's just the sort of thing they leave out – printers have taken more years off my life than pulmonary congestion, I can tell you. Send "Buffalo" to *Blackwood's* and "Pearl" to *Transition*, and if you get a pound for them put it in the Sacha Fund.'

PIKE: The reference is obscure.

FLORA: 'I'm writing this at my table on the verandah, looking longingly to the hills I can't see. The dak menagerie is subdued by the heat, except for a pi-dog barking under the house – and I'd better start with what interrupted me yesterday after my early morning ride – which was a Rolls Royce *circa* 1912 but brand new, as it were, driven by a Sikh in a turban called Singh – '

PIKE: A tautology: all Sikhs are named Singh (however, not all people named Singh are Sikhs).

FLORA: Oh, shut up! (*She is shouting at the dog, which is responding. She manages to get rid of the dog – clapping her hands and generally making a dog-dismissing row. The dog departs, whining and yelping.*)
'He was a chauffeur with a note from His Highness the

63

Rajah of Jummapur, inquiring after my health and assuring me that the spiritual beauty of Jummapur had been increased a thousandfold by my presence, and asking my indulgence towards his undistinguished collection of motor cars, which nevertheless might be worthy of my interest during an idle hour since he understood I was a connoisseur of the automobile . . . Well, what is a poor girl to do? Hop into the back of the Rolls, that's what.'
(*Sound of* FLORA *getting into the Rolls.*)
Thank you!
(*The car moves, etc.*)
'The Rajah's palace didn't exactly have a garage, more of a cavalry barracks with the Motor Show thrown in, and he himself was there to greet me.'

RAJAH: Miss Crewe! How delightful that you were able to come!

FLORA: Oh, how sweet of you to ask me . . . your Highness . . . oh – sorry!

RAJAH: Please!

FLORA: 'And I made a mess of that, sticking my hand out at his bow, bowing at his hand – '
What a wonderful sight!
' – but he was very sporting about it, and there were all these cars gleaming in the courtyard – with a dozen grooms standing by, one couldn't think of them as mechanics.'

RAJAH: Let me show you one or two.

FLORA: Thank you! Oh – a Hispano-Suiza!
'He's a large soft-looking man with beautiful eyes like a seal and wearing a long buttoned-up brocade coat over white leggings, no jewellery except a yellow diamond ring not much bigger than my engagement ring from Gus, only real, I suppose – '

PIKE: Augustus de Boucheron enjoyed brief celebrity as a millionaire philanthropist and patron of the arts. FC met him, and received his proposal of marriage, on October 11th 1918, at a party given for the Russian Ballet by the Sitwells at Swan Walk (it was at the same party that Maynard Keynes met the ballerina Lopokova). FC had returned from France only hours earlier and was wearing her auxiliary nurse's uniform. Her fortunes were at their lowest ebb, for she was supporting her sister, still at school, and also her father, who, since being invalided out of the Army, had given up the Bar and enjoyed few periods of lucidity. The engagement to de Boucheron was announced on January 1st 1919 and ended on August 1st in a furniture store (see note on page 334).

FLORA: ' – and he knew very little about cars, he just liked the look of them, which was endearing, and I know how badly this must be going down in Doughty Street but we soon got on to politics – he was at school with Winston Churchill.'

RAJAH: But I'm afraid I can't remember him at all. Look at this one! I couldn't resist the headlamps! So enormous, like the eggs of a mythical bird!

FLORA: Yes – a Brancusi!

RAJAH: Is it? I don't know their names. All the same, I read Churchill's speeches with great interest. He is right in what he says, don't you agree, Miss Crewe? The loss of India would reduce Britain to a minor power.

FLORA: That may be, but one must consider India's interests too.

RAJAH: But what about Jummapur's interests?

FLORA: Yes, of course, but aren't they same thing?

RAJAH: No, no. Independence would be the beginning of the end for the Native States. Though in a sense you are right too – Independence may be the beginning of the end for Indian nationalism too. Only yesterday, you may have heard about the hullabaloo in town.

FLORA: Yes.

RAJAH: The Princes stood firm with the British during the First Uprising in my grandfather's day –

FLORA: The . . . ?

RAJAH: In '57 the danger was from fundamentalists –

FLORA: The Mutiny . . .

RAJAH: – today it is the progressives. Marxism. Civil disobedience. But I told the Viceroy, you have to fight them the same way, you won't win by playing cricket. (*He presses a bulb-horn, which honks*.) My father drove this one. It's a Bentley.

FLORA: Yes.

RAJAH: He won it at Monte Carlo. He spent much of his time in the south of France, for his health. (*He laughs*.) But *you* have come to India for *your* health!

FLORA: (*Not pleased*) Well . . . yes, your Highness. Everybody seems to know everything about me.

RAJAH: Should we have some refreshment? (*He opens the door of a car*.)

FLORA: (*Puzzled*) Oh . . . thank you.

RAJAH: After you.

FLORA: You mean in the car?

RAJAH: Do you like this one?

FLORA: I . . . yes, of course. It's a Packard.

RAJAH: It's quite a step to my apartments. Why walk in the sun when we have so many motorcars?

FLORA: Oh I see. Thank you. (*She gets into the car*.)

RAJAH: I keep them all ready. Would you care to drive?

FLORA: Yes, I'd love to. I'll slip over.

(*She moves over to the steering wheel. The* RAJAH *gets into the car and closes the door*.)

RAJAH: Jolly good, we'll have some tiffin. When do you leave Jummapur?

FLORA: ' – and we drove all of two hundred yards past saluting sentries, into the palace proper, which had a fountain inside, and we walked through a series of little gardens into his reception room, where we had sherbet – you can imagine the rest, can't you? – me sat on silk cushions being peeped at by giggling ladies of the harem through the latticework of carved marble – well, no such thing. We had tea and cold cuts and little iced cakes, and the furniture was from Heals, three-piece suite and all, and I know it was Heals because the sofa was absolutely the one I broke my engagement on when I took Gus to the French Pictures – my God, I thought, that's the Modigliani sofa!'

PIKE: The exhibition of Modern French Art at Heal and Sons in the Tottenham Court Road enlivened the hot early-August

66

days of 1919. Modigliani was one of several newer artists shown with the better-known Matisse, Picasso and Derain, and it was his nudes, including the 'Peasant Girl', now in the Tate Gallery, which provoked such comments in the press as that the show was glorying in prostitution. FC had met Modigliani in Paris at his first show, on December 3rd 1917 (the date is fixed by the fact that the show was closed by the police on the opening day) and she sat, or rather reclined, for the artist soon afterwards. Concurrently with the French pictures, Messrs Heals were showing a model flat. FC arrived at Heals with de Boucheron, expecting to see her portrait, only to discover that her fiancé had bought the painting from the artist and, as he triumphantly confessed, burned it. The ensuing row moved from the gallery to the model flat, and it was on the sofa of the model sitting-room that FC returned de Boucheron's engagement ring (though not the lease on the Flood Street house, which was to be the Crewes' London home from then on). De Boucheron, under his real name, Perkins Butcher, went to prison in 1925 for issuing a false prospectus. His end is unknown.

FLORA: 'I started to tell his Highness about Heals but when I said French pictures he got hold of the wrong end of the stick entirely – '

RAJAH: French pictures?

FLORA: Yes. There was a tremendous fuss – the pictures were wallowing in prostitution, that sort of thing. And of course those of us who defended them were simply admitting our depravity!

RAJAH: My dear Miss Crewe, you are quite the emancipated woman!

FLORA: Not at all. What has being a woman got to do with it?

RAJAH: Oh, I agree with you! I was guilty of male prejudice!

FLORA: In fact they are probably more to my taste than yours – surely it's more a matter of culture than gender?

RAJAH: Ah, but we have 'French pictures' of our own. Of course, you have never seen them.

FLORA: I'm not sure that I understand.

67

RAJAH: In *our* culture, you see, erotic art has a long history and a most serious purpose. (*Walking away*.) These drawings, for example – if I may be so bold – are the depictions not of depravity . . . (*walking back*) but of precepts towards a proper fulfilment of that side of life which . . .

FLORA: 'And he produced an album of exquisite water colours – medieval, I think – which we admired solemnly together, he determined to acknowledge me as an enlightened woman, I determined to be one. Really what a muddle, and not entirely honest, of course – he insisted I chose one as a gift – '

No, really, I couldn't –

RAJAH: Yes, yes – which one would you like?

FLORA: ' – like pondering a big box of chocolates – should one go for the Turkish Delight or plump for the nut cluster?' Well, this one is rather sweet . . .

RAJAH: Ah, yes . . .

FLORA: How very kind.

' – and he invited me to move into the palace for the remainder of my visit but I got away finally in a yellow Studebaker and was brought home at lamp-lighting time . . .'

(*Sounds of the Studebaker arriving, Flora getting out and closing the car door; the car leaving.* FLORA *calls out.*)

Thank you very much, Mr Singh! (*She comes up the wooden steps to the verandah.*) Oh, Mr Das!

DAS: Good evening, Miss Crewe! I'm sorry if we frightened you.

FLORA: And Mr Coomaraswami!

COOMARASWAMI: Yes, it is me, Miss Crewe.

FLORA: Good evening. What a surprise.

COOMARASWAMI: I assure you – I beg you – we have not come to presume on your hospitality –

FLORA: I wish I had some whisky to offer you, but will you come inside.

COOMARASWAMI: It will be cooler for you to remain on the verandah.

FLORA: Let me find Nazrul.

COOMARASWAMI: He is not here, evidently. But perhaps now

that the mistress has returned it is permitted to light the lamp?

FLORA: Yes, of course.

COOMARASWAMI: So much more pleasant than sitting in the electric light. (*He lights the oil lamp.*) There we are. And the moon will clear the house tops in a few minutes . . . but where is it? Perhaps on the wrong side of the house. Never mind.

FLORA: Please sit down.

COOMARASWAMI: May I take this chair?

FLORA: No, that's Mr Das's chair. And this is mine. So that leaves you with the sofa.

COOMARASWAMI: Ah, never, never has my fatness received more charming, more delicate acknowledgement! (*He sits down.*) Oh yes, very comfortable. Thank you, Miss Crewe. Mr Das told me that I was exceeding our rights of acquaintance with you in coming to see you without proper arrangement, and even more so to lie in wait for you like *mulaquatis*. If it is so, he is blameless. Please direct your displeasure to me.

DAS: Miss Crewe does not understand *mulaquatis*.

COOMARASWAMI: Petitioners!

FLORA: In my house you are always friends.

COOMARASWAMI: Mr Das, what did I tell you!

FLORA: But what can I do for you?

DAS: Nothing at all! We require nothing!

FLORA: Oh . . .

COOMARASWAMI: Have you had a pleasant day, Miss Crewe?

FLORA: Extremely interesting. I have been visiting his Highness the Rajah.

COOMARASWAMI: My goodness!

FLORA: I believe you knew that, Mr Coomaraswami.

COOMARASWAMI: Oh, you have found me out!

FLORA: He showed me his cars . . . and we had an interesting conversation, about art . . .

COOMARASWAMI: And poetry, of course.

FLORA: And politics.

COOMARASWAMI: Politics, yes. I hope, we both hope – that

your association with, that our association with, in fact – if we caused you embarrassment, if you thought for a moment that I personally would have knowingly brought upon you, compromised you, by association with –

FLORA: Stop, stop. Mr Das, I am going to ask *you*. What is the matter?

DAS: The matter?

FLORA: I shall be absolutely furious in a moment.

DAS: Yes, yes, quite so. My friend Coomaraswami, speaking as President of the Theosophical Society, wishes to say that if his Highness reproached you or engaged you in any unwelcome conversation regarding your connection with the Society, he feels responsible, and yet at the same time wishes you to know that –

FLORA: His Highness never mentioned the Theosophical Society.

DAS: Ah.

COOMARASWAMI: Not at all, Miss Crewe?

FLORA: Not at all.

COOMARASWAMI: Oh . . . well, jolly good!

FLORA: What has happened?

COOMARASWAMI: Ah well, it is really of no interest. I am very sorry to have mentioned it. And we must leave you, it was not right to trouble you after all. Will you come, Mr Das?

FLORA: I hope it is nothing to do with my lecture?

COOMARASWAMI: (*Getting up*) Oh no! Certainly not!

DAS: Nothing!

COOMARASWAMI: Mr Das said we should not mention the thing, and how truly he spoke. I am sorry. Goodnight, Miss Crewe. (*He shouts towards somebody distant, in Urdu, and the explanation is an approaching jingle of harness, horse and buggy. He goes down the steps to meet it and climbs aboard.*)

DAS: I am coming, Mr Coomaraswami. Please wait for me a moment.

FLORA: If you expect to be my friends, you must behave like friends and not like whatever-you-called it. Tell me what has happened.

70

COOMARASWAMI: (*Off*) Mr Das!

DAS: (*Shouts*) Please wait!

FLORA: Well?

DAS: The Theosophical Society has been banned, you see. The order came to Mr Coomaraswami's house last night.

FLORA: But why?

DAS: Because of the disturbances in the town.

FLORA: The riot?

DAS: Yes, the riot.

FLORA: I know about it. The Hindus wanted the Muslims to close their shops. What has that to do with the Theosophical Society?

COOMARASWAMI: (*Off*) I am going, Mr Das!

DAS: (*Shouts*) I come now!

Mr Coomaraswami is a man with many hats! And his Highness the Rajah is not a nationalist. I must leave you, Miss Crewe. But may I step inside to fetch my painting away?

FLORA: If you like.

DAS: I do not have my bicycle this evening, so I can manage the easel also.

FLORA: Mr Das, did you tell people I was ill?

DAS: What do you mean?

FLORA: That I came to India for my health?

COOMARASWAMI: (*Off*) I cannot wait, Mr Das!

DAS: (*Shouts*) A moment!

Why do you ask me that?

FLORA: He is leaving you behind.

(*The horse and buggy are heard departing.*)

DAS: I will walk, then.

FLORA: It seems that everyone from the Rajah to the Resident knows all about me. I told no one except you. If I want people to know things, I tell them myself, you see. I'm sorry to mention it but if there's something wrong between two friends I always think it is better to say what it is.

DAS: Oh . . . my dear Miss Crewe . . . it was known long before you arrived in Jummapur. Mr Chamberlain's letter said exactly why you were coming. Mr Coomaraswami told me himself when I began to paint your portrait. But, you see, I already knew from talking with others. This is how it is with us, I'm afraid. The information was not considered to be private, only something to be treated with tact.

FLORA: Oh . . .

DAS: As for the Rajah and the Resident, I am sure they knew before anybody. A letter from England to Mr Coomaraswami would certainly be opened.

FLORA: Oh . . . (*She is merely making sounds, close to tears.*)

DAS: You must not blame yourself. Please.

FLORA: Oh, Mr Das . . . I'm so glad . . . and so sorry. Oh dear, have you got a hanky?

DAS: Yes . . . certainly . . .

FLORA: Thank you. How stupid I am.

(DAS *opens the door to the interior.*)

DAS: I will fetch the canvas.

(*We go with him. He moves the easel, folds it, etc.*)

FLORA: (*Off*) Don't take it.

(*Approaching.*) If it is still a gift, I would like to keep it, just as it is.

DAS: Unfinished?

FLORA: Yes. All portraits should be unfinished. Otherwise it's like looking at a stopped clock. Your handkerchief smells faintly of . . . something nice. Is it cinnamon?

DAS: Possibly not. The portrait is yours, if you would like it. Of course. I must take it off the frame for you, or it will not travel easily in your luggage. Perhaps I can find a knife in the kitchen, to take out the little nails.

FLORA: There are scissors on the table.

DAS: Ah – yes. Thank you. No – I think I would damage them. May I call Nazrul?

FLORA: I thought –

DAS: Yes – Mr Coomaraswami sent him away, he is suspicious of everyone. I'm sorry.

FLORA: It doesn't matter.

DAS: No. There is no hurry.

FLORA: No. But I am leaving tomorrow.

DAS: Tomorrow?

FLORA: I think I must. Every day seems hotter than the day before. Even at dawn.

DAS: Yes, you are right of course.

FLORA: But I will see you again, because I'll come back this way to Bombay, by July 10th at the latest. My boat sails on the 12th.

DAS: You may take a later boat.

FLORA: No, I cannot. My sister . . . oh, you'll be horrified, but never mind; my sister is having a baby in October.

DAS: That is joyful news.

FLORA: Oh, good.

DAS: I can keep the painting for you until you come back if you like.

FLORA: No, I'd like to have it with me.

DAS: Miss Crewe . . . actually I have brought something to show you. I decided I must not show it to you after all, but if we are friends again . . . I would like you to see it.

FLORA: What is it?

DAS: I left it in my briefcase outside.

FLORA: I would like to see it.

DAS: (*Hesitates*) Well . . . I will bring it.

FLORA: All right.

(DAS *walks the few steps back to the verandah, and returns, speaking.*)

DAS: I have wrapped it, although it is itself only a sheet of paper.

FLORA: Oh . . . shall I open it?

DAS: You must look at it in the light. Let me –

FLORA: No – not the electric light. I seldom cry, but never in the electric light. Do you mind? There is enough light in the other window; Mr Coomaraswami was quite right about the moon. (*She moves. She unwraps the paper.*) It's going to be a drawing, isn't it? Oh!

DAS: (*Nervous, bright*) Yes! A good joke, is it not? A Rajput miniature, by Nirad Das!

FLORA: (*Not heeding him*) Oh . . . it's the most beautiful thing . . .

73

DAS: (*Brightly*) I'm so pleased you like it! A quite witty
     pastiche –
FLORA: (*Heeding him now*) Are you going to be Indian? Please
     don't.
DAS: (*Heeding her*) I . . . I am Indian.
FLORA: An Indian artist.
DAS: Yes.
FLORA: Yes. This one is for yourself.
DAS: You are not offended?
FLORA: No, I'm pleased. It has *rasa*.
DAS: I think so. Yes. I hope so.
FLORA: I forget its name.
DAS: (*Pause*) Shringara.
FLORA: Yes. Shringara. The *rasa* of erotic love. Whose god is
     Vishnu.
DAS: Yes.
FLORA: Whose colour is blue-black.
DAS: Shyama. Yes.
FLORA: It seemed a strange colour for love.
DAS: Krishna was often painted shyama.
FLORA: Yes. I can see that now. It's the colour he looked in the
     moonlight.

MRS SWAN: 'Which only goes to show, when in Rome, etc., and I wish I'd remembered that when I *was* in Rome. Interrupted! Next day. Oh dear, guess what? You won't approve. Quite right. So I think it's time to go. Love 'em and leave 'em . . .'

ANISH: May I see?

MRS SWAN: It's no different from what you can read in the book. Though it's a relief not to have Clark Gable butting in all the time. I decided not to tell Mr Pike about Rome, even though it was several Popes ago and Norman Douglas wouldn't have given a hoot. Let sleeping dogs lie, that's what I say.

ANISH: 'You won't approve . . . Oh dear, guess what? You won't approve . . .'

MRS SWAN: I wish I'd kept the envelopes, they'd be worth something now to a collector, a philatelist, I mean.

ANISH: Mr Pike's footnote talks about the political agent, Captain Durance.

MRS SWAN: Gratuitously.

ANISH: Yes! Why wouldn't you approve of Captain Durance? Surely it's more likely she meant . . .

MRS SWAN: Meant what, Mr Das?

ANISH: I don't mean any offence.

MRS SWAN: Then you must take care not to give it.

ANISH: Would you have disapproved of a British Army officer – Mrs Swan? – more than an Indian painter?

MRS SWAN: Certainly. Mr Pike is spot-on there. In 1930 I was working for a Communist newspaper. Which goes to show that people are surprising. But you know that from your father, don't you?

ANISH: Why?

MRS SWAN: He must have surprised you too. The thorn in the lion's paw.

ANISH: Yes. Yes, I was surprised.

MRS SWAN: In any case, if you read Flora's words simply for what they say, you would see that when she said I wouldn't *approve*, she did not mean this man or that man. Flora was ill. As it turned out she was dying. Cigarettes, whisky and men, and for that matter the hundred-yard dash, were not on the menu. She didn't need Dr Guppy to tell her that. No, I would not have approved. But Flora's weakness was always romance. To call it that.

ANISH: She had a romance with my father, then.

MRS SWAN: Quite possibly. Or with Captain Durance. Or his Highness the Rajah of Jummapur. Or someone else entirely. It hardly matters, looking back. Men were not really important to Flora. If they had been, they would have been fewer. She used them like batteries. When things went flat, she'd put in a new one.

FLORA: 'Sweat collects and holds as a pearl at my throat,
    lets go and slides like a tongue-tip
    down a Modigliani,
    spills into the delta, now in the salt-lick,
    lost in the mangroves and the airless moisture,
    a seed-pearl returning to the oyster –
    et nos cedamus amori –
    (*She is on the verandah, at dawn. The Daimler car is
    approaching.*)
    (*Hearing the car*) Oh . . .
    (*The Daimler arrives. The engine is cut, the car door opens.*)
    David . . . ?
DURANCE: You're up!
FLORA: Up with the dawn. What on earth are *you* doing?
DURANCE: (*Approaching*) I'm afraid I came to wake you. Don't
    you sleep?
FLORA: Yes, I slept early and woke early.
DURANCE: The grapevine says you're leaving today.
FLORA: Yes.
DURANCE: I promised you a turn with the Daimler –
    remember?
FLORA: Yes.
DURANCE: I wanted to show you the sunrise. There's a pretty
    place for it only ten minutes down the road. Will you
    come?
FLORA: Can I go in my dressing-gown?
DURANCE: Well . . . better not.
FLORA: Righto. I'll get dressed.
DURANCE: Good.
FLORA: Come up.
    (DURANCE *comes up the verandah steps.*)
DURANCE: Writing a poem?
FLORA: Writing *out* a poem, to send to my sister.
    (*Going.*) I'll be quick.

DURANCE: The damnedest thing happened to me just now.

FLORA: (*Inside*) Can't hear you! Come in, it's quite safe.

(DURANCE *also enters the interior. He is now in the living-room.* FLORA *is further within the bungalow.*)

DURANCE: That fellow Das was on the road. I'm sure it was him.

FLORA: (*Off*) Well . . . why not?

DURANCE: He cut me.

FLORA: (*Off*) What?

DURANCE: I gave him a wave and he turned his back. I thought – 'Well, that's a first!'

FLORA: (*Further off*) Oh! There's hope for him yet.

DURANCE: They'll be throwing stones next.

What did you say?

FLORA: (*Off*) Wait – I'm going into the shower!

DURANCE: Oh. Do you want any help?

FLORA: (*Further off*) No, thank you, not today. (*After a few moments the shower is turned off.*)

(*In the bathroom*) Oh – yes, I do – my towel is in there – will you bung it on the bed?

(DURANCE *does this. He enters the bedroom.* FLORA's *voice is still beyond a closed door.*)

DURANCE: It's very damp.

FLORA: Yes. Second shower today. Out you go.

DURANCE: Oh . . . !

FLORA: What?

DURANCE: You're reading Emily Eden. I read it years ago.

FLORA: We'll miss the sunrise.

DURANCE: (*With the book*) There's a bit somewhere . . . she reminds me of you. 'Off with their heads!'

FLORA: (*Off*) Whose heads? Are you out?

(DURANCE *leaves the bedroom and enters the living-room.*)

DURANCE: Yes, I'm out. I'll see if I can find it.

(*Now* FLORA *is in the bedroom.*)

FLORA: (*Off*) I'll be two shakes.

DURANCE: Here it is – listen! – 'Simla, Saturday, May 25th, 1839. The Queen's Ball "came off" yesterday with great success . . .' Oh!

FLORA: (*Off*) What!

DURANCE: Nothing. I found your bookmark.

FLORA: (*Off*) Oh . . . (*Now she enters the living-room.*) I'm sort of decent – wet hair will have to do. It's not my bookmark – I put it in the book for safekeeping.

DURANCE: Where did you get such a thing?

FLORA: His Highness gave it to me.

DURANCE: Why?

FLORA: (*Reacting to his tone*) Because he is a Rajah. Because he was feeling generous. Because he hoped I'd go to bed with him. I don't know.

DURANCE: But how could he . . . feel himself in such intimacy with you? Had you met him before?

FLORA: No, David – it was a muddle –

DURANCE: But my dear girl, in accepting a gift like this don't you see – (*Pause.*) Well, it's your look-out, of course . . .

FLORA: Shall we go?

DURANCE: . . . but I'm in a frightfully difficult position now.

FLORA: Why?

DURANCE: Did he visit you?

FLORA: I visited him.

DURANCE: I know. Did he visit you?

FLORA: Mind your own business.

DURANCE: But it is my business.

FLORA: Because you think you love me?

DURANCE: No, I . . . Keeping tabs on what his Highness is up to is one of my . . . I mean I write reports to Delhi.

FLORA: (*Amused*) Oh, heavens!

DURANCE: You're a politically sensitive person, actually, by association with Chamberlain . . . I mean this sort of thing –

FLORA: Oh, darling policeman.

DURANCE: How can I ignore it?

FLORA: Don't ignore it. Report what you like. I don't mind, you see. *You* mind. But I don't. I have never minded. (*She steps on to the verandah.*)
(*In despair*) Oh – look at the sky! We're going to be too late!

DURANCE: (*To hell with it*) Come on! Our road is due west – if
  you know how to drive a car we'll make it.
  (*They dash to the car, which roars into life and takes off at
  what sounds like a dangerous speed.*)
FLORA: 'My suitor came to say goodbye, and now I'm packed,
  portrait and all, and waiting for Mr Coomaraswami to take
  me to the station in his chariot. I'll post this in Jaipur as
  soon as I get there – I'm not going to post it here because
  I'm not. I feel fit as two lops this morning, and happy too,
  because something good happened here which made me
  feel half-way better about Modi and Gus and getting back
  to Paris too late – a sin which I'll carry to my grave.'
PIKE: This appears to be about the portrait. FC had arranged to
  return to France to sit for Modigliani in the autumn of
  1919, but she delayed, arriving only on the morning of
  January 23rd, unaware that Modigliani had been taken to
  hospital. He died on the following evening without
  regaining consciousness, of tuberculosis, aged thirty-five.
  Thus, the frontispiece of this book shows the only known
  portrait of Flora Crewe, by an unknown Indian artist.

MRS SWAN *opens her front door from inside.*

MRS SWAN: Goodbye, Mr Das.

ANISH: Goodbye, Mrs Swan – thank you.

MRS SWAN: If you change your mind, I'm sure Flora wouldn't
mind . . .

ANISH: No. Thank you, but it's my father I'm thinking of. He
really wouldn't want it, not even in a footnote. So we'll say
nothing to Mr Pike.

MRS SWAN: Well, don't put it away in a trunk either.

ANISH: Oh no! It will be on the wall at home, and I'll tell my
children too. Thank you for tea – the Victoria sponge was
best!

MRS SWAN: I'm baking again tomorrow. I still have raspberries
left to pick and the plums to come, look. I always loved the
fruit trees at home. (*Walking from front door to the gate. A
quiet street.*)

ANISH: At home?

MRS SWAN: Orchards of apricot – almond – plum – I never
cared for the southern fruits, mango, paw-paw and such
like. But up in the North-West . . . I was quite unprepared
for it when I first arrived. It was early summer. There was
a wind blowing.

(*Cross-fading, wind.*)

And I have never seen such blossom, it blew everywhere,
there were drifts of snow-white flowers piled up against the
walls of the graveyard. I had to kneel on the ground and
sweep the petals off her stone to read her name.

NELL: 'Florence Edith Crewe . . . Born March 21st 1895 . . .
Died June 10th 1930. *Requiescat In Pacem.*'

FRANCIS: I'm afraid it's very simple. I hope that's all right.

NELL: Yes. It was good of you.

FRANCIS: Oh no, we look after our own. Of course.

NELL: I think she would have liked 'Poet' under her name. If I
left some money here to pay for it . . . ?

FRANCIS: There are funds within my discretion. You may count
on it, Miss Crewe. Poet. I should have thought of that. It is
how *we* remember your sister.

NELL: Really?

FRANCIS: She read one evening. The Club has a habit of asking
guests to sing for their supper and Miss Crewe read to us
. . . from her work.

NELL: Oh dear.

FRANCIS: (*Laughs gently*) Yes. Well, we're a bit behind the
times, I expect. But we all liked her very much. We didn't
know what to expect because we understood she was a
protégée of Mr Chamberlain, who had lectured in the town
some years before. Perhaps you know him.

NELL: Yes. I'm not really in touch with him nowadays.

FRANCIS: Ah. It was just about this time of year when she
was here, wasn't it? It was clear she wasn't well – these
steps we just climbed, for instance, she could hardly
manage them. Even so. Death in India is often more
unexpected, despite being more common, if you
understand me. I'm talking far too much. I'm so sorry.
I'll wait at the gate. Please stay as long as you wish, I have
no one waiting for me.

NELL: I won't be a moment. Flora didn't like mopers.
(FRANCIS *leaves her.*)
(*Quietly*) Bye bye, darling . . . oh – damn! (. . . *because she
has burst into sobs. She weeps unrestrainedly.*)

FRANCIS: (*Returning*) Oh . . . oh, I say . . .

NELL: Oh, I'm sorry.

FRANCIS: No – please . . . can I . . . ?

(NELL *stops crying after a few moments*.)

NELL: I've messed up your coat. I've got a hanky somewhere.

FRANCIS: Would you like to . . . ? Here . . .

NELL: Yes. Thank you. (*She uses his handkerchief*.) I came too soon after all. I hated waiting a whole year but . . . well, anyway. Thank you, it's a bit wet. Should I keep it? Oh, look, I've found mine, we can swap.

FRANCIS: Don't you worry about anything. What a shame you had to come on your own. You have another sister, I believe. Or a brother?

NELL: No. Why?

FRANCIS: Oh. Flora was anxious to return to England to be an aunt, she said.

NELL: Yes. I had a baby in October. He only lived a little while, unfortunately. There was something wrong.

FRANCIS: Oh. I'm so sorry.

NELL: It's why I couldn't come before.

FRANCIS: Yes, I see. What rotten luck. What was his name?

NELL: Alexander. Sacha Alexander Percival Crewe. How nice of you to ask. Nobody ever does. I say, how about that blossom!

(*They start to walk*.)

FRANCIS: Yes, it's quite a spot, isn't it? I hope you stay a while. First time in India?

NELL: Yes.

FRANCIS: Mind the loose stone here. May I . . . ?

NELL: Thank you. I'm sorry I blubbed, Mr Swan.

FRANCIS: I won't tell anyone. Do call me Francis, by the way. Nobody calls me Mr Swan.

NELL: Francis, then.

FRANCIS: Do you like cricket?

NELL: (*Laughs*) Well, I don't play a *lot*.

FRANCIS: There's a match tomorrow.

NELL: *Here?*

FRANCIS: Oh, yes. We're going to field a Test team next year, you know.

NELL: We?
FRANCIS: India.
NELL: Oh.

EMILY EDEN: 'Simla, Saturday, May 25th, 1839. The Queen's
Ball "came off" yesterday with great success . . . Between
the two tents there was a boarded platform for dancing,
roped and arched in with flowers and then in different parts
of the valley, wherever the trees would allow of it, there
was "Victoria", "God Save The Queen" and "Candahar"
in immense letters twelve feet high. There was a very old
Hindu temple also prettily lit up. Vishnu, to whom I
believe it really belonged, must have been affronted. We
dined at six, then had fireworks, and coffee, and then they
all danced till twelve. It was the most beautiful evening;
such a moon, and the mountains looked so soft and *grave*,
after all the fireworks and glare. Twenty years ago no
European had ever been here, and there we were with a
band playing, and observing that St Cloup's Potage à la
Julienne was perhaps better than his other soups, and that
some of the ladies' sleeves were too tight according to the
overland fashions for March, and so on, and all this in the
face of those high hills, and we one hundred and five
Europeans being surrounded by at least three thousand
mountaineers, who, wrapped up in their hill blankets,
looked on at what we call our polite amusements, and
bowed to the ground if a European came near them. I
sometimes wonder they do not cut all our heads off and say
nothing more about it.'